early years
training &
management

Manager's handbook

D1103478

June O'Sullivan

Editor	Author	Illustrations
Jane Bishop	June O'Sullivan	Adrian Barclay/Beehive Illustration
Assistant Editor	**Series Designer**	**Cover artwork**
Saveria Mezzana	Mark Udall	© Ingram Publishing
	Designer	
	Erik Ivens	

Acknowledgements

Her Majesty's Stationery Office and Queen's Printer for Scotland for the use of material from *NVQ/SVQ in Management Level 3* produced by MCI with funding from the Department for Education and Employment © 2000, Crown copyright.

Pauline Kenyon for assistance in the writing of Chapter 9.

Every effort has been made to trace copyright holders and the publishers apologise for any inadvertent omissions.

Contents

Contents

Chapter 1 The early years manager

> ➤ **Who is the early years manager?**
> ➤ **The manager as a leader**
> ➤ **The manager as a planner**
> ➤ **The manager as an organiser**
> ➤ **The manager as an effective communicator**
> ➤ **The manager as a team builder**
> ➤ **The manager as a motivator**
> ➤ **The manager as a decision-maker**
> ➤ **The role of the manager as teacher**
> ➤ **The manager as supervisor**
> ➤ **NVQ in Management Level 3**

Who is the early years manager?

Staff in early years settings are generally promoted to managerial posts because they have shown themselves to be able childcare practitioners with the potential to develop the setting, the curriculum, the staff and themselves.

However, becoming a manager is just the first step of an unnervingly steep learning curve and new managers often find the transition from confident practitioner, sometimes with little or no immediate support, to be very difficult. It is not unusual to hear new managers saying, 'It's much easier being with the children, managing adults is a nightmare'. Many experienced managers can remember feeling this way but they will, by then, have gone through the induction process, matured into the job and reached a level of competence where they feel comfortable with their role and can transfer their learning to a range of situations.

Management is a combination of theory and practice that is designed to ensure that the work of an organisation is developed, supported and guided by an individual or team so as to effectively meet the organisation's purpose. Some people are considered to be 'born managers'; they appear to have an instinctive grasp of management theory and expertise. This is rare however, and most managers need to actively learn management skills.

The role of a manager is a complex one requiring an ability to use and develop a range of skills in a variety of contexts.

The manager as a leader

One of the most important aspects of management is leadership. Some people are considered to be natural leaders but others argue that the main principles of leadership can be learned. What has been found is that while it is possible to identify what makes effective leaders successful, the ingredients of success are very hard to teach.

Leaders are expected to be able to share a vision that gives their staff a sense of purpose and worth, so that they know where they fit into an organisation and how their contributions are recognised and valued. As a leader, you need to show that you can get things done, make change happen and evaluate successes and failures with painful honesty. According to Shackleton, leader of the great polar expedition in 1916, leaders have to make sure that the whole job is done. Your staff may call it quits after the heavy lifting is over, but the leader is responsible for seeing the work through to its successful conclusion.

How do you do this?

➤ Identify a clear vision for the future (sometimes written as a mission statement): 'The best local play service in the borough'.

➤ Reaffirm your purpose: to offer low cost out of school service.

➤ Agree on the values that underpin your purpose (the way that we do things here): 'Play is key', 'Children need physical play every day indoors and outside' and 'Links with parents are vital'.

➤ Involve the staff so that you all agree on how you are going to achieve your aims: staff meetings, working groups, lead responsibilities, updates and other ways of keeping people informed.

➤ Inspire, influence, and motivate the team to want to achieve the objectives and have clear action plans.

➤ Monitor and review the progress (the results should link the vision and purpose to the next stage of the planning process) and make the necessary changes to keep you on course and help you to identify how you recognise success.

To be a leader you must be willing to continually learn about yourself; successful managers know their strengths and limitations. As a manager, you are responsible for creating an environment of self-development (see Chapter 2) for your staff, but you must also remember to develop your own skills. Check that you are comfortable with all areas of your job by devising an induction programme, based on your job description, with key management responsibilities highlighted. Even if you do not have a line manager, you can use this information to develop your own personal plan (see the sample induction form on the photocopiable sheet 'Induction for new managers' on page 136).

Successful leaders have breadth and emotional maturity; they are more shock-proof than other people and are neither over-elated by success nor crushed by

failure. Those in the early years sector could be described as reflective practitioners, and they are able to consider the impact of what they do on both staff and children in their setting. Early years managers can have a significant coaching role as they advise and support while they work alongside staff, extending thinking and supporting good practice. In addition to setting up systems, such as regular staff meetings, supervision and daily feedback sessions, these managers support staff to share knowledge and introduce ideas, helping the whole team to develop and improve practice.

Leaders need to show integrity and credibility, building up trust with staff by keeping promises, showing humility if they get things wrong, listening actively, acknowledging and thanking staff and 'walking the talk' – in other words, showing their values in everything that they do. As a leader, actions definitely speak louder than words.

Knowing others is intelligence; knowing yourself is true wisdom; mastering others is strength; mastering yourself is true power.

– Lao Tze –

Providing care in the early years is a people-intensive service, so managers need to apply very effective leadership and communication skills in order to create a motivating and creative environment. This can be difficult, given that many early years managers are not solely in managerial roles but have this responsibility in addition to their requirement to work directly with the children, as part of the daily routine. Sometimes managers prefer to be part of the daily routine, rather than accept their leadership responsibilities for looking forward and planning for the future of the organisation. On the other hand, working directly with the staff is the best way to see what exactly goes on.

The manager as a planner

Good planning is a good management tool. You must be able to plan to provide the daily care service, but you also need to be able to understand how to strategically plan ahead if you want the setting to survive, develop and grow.

Having a shared philosophy is crucial, and the manager must have a sound and up-to-date knowledge of what is expected and must then be able to articulate this to all staff, parents, carers and external agencies. For example, if the ethos of your setting is that children learn best in a happy, friendly, child-centred environment, where the routine is geared to meet their needs, then the manager has to make this happen by creating an organisational framework to ensure that this ethos is delivered.

Having planned to ensure that the service runs on a daily basis, you can begin to look to the future. You will need to be flexible, as managers, especially those in the early years, have to keep aware of the impact that economic and demographic changes could bring. The sector has faced a recruitment shortage at a time of Government-driven childcare expansion. These changes require managers to respond flexibly and creatively, while still meeting their statutory responsibilities.

The plans that you make have to be easily understood by everyone involved in their implementation. They are also more likely to become operational if staff are engaged in their preparation and delivery. Managers need to know the strategies for agreeing and meeting planning targets, such as SWOT analysis, SMART targets, action plans and evaluation check-lists (see Chapters 2, 7 and 10).

Having identified what is needed and created suitable action plans, you need to monitor information about how the plans are working in order to judge whether they are effective. You can then measure the key factors that contributed to the success, and this may influence how you develop the service and influence practice and knowledge of your staff. The process itself can contribute to creating an environment where staff are reflective.

The manager as an organiser

Efficient administrative systems are essential because they put in place a series of procedures, which can ensure the smooth daily operation of the setting. An inefficient manager creates a dependency, which means that only they know how to do certain things. Systems for managing the waiting-list, planning the routine, managing group activities and responding to emergencies are critical if staff members are to be empowered and able to respond to situations as they arise. Every organised office will have a set of operational procedures, which are easily identified, standardised if they cover more than one setting, and regularly checked and updated.

One of your administrative tasks as a manager is to manage a budget and avoid financial mismanagement (see Chapter 7). This requires you to provide an accurate picture of where and when resources are being used at any time. It is also the basis for forecasting finance needs to meet future targets. It is important to support the staff team to understand that finance is a limited commodity by involving them in stocktaking, auditing resources and financial planning.

Annual development plans are a useful means of helping both you and your team to agree on the main annual expenditure. This will cover which items you need to replace, such as paints, paper, sand, cleaning materials, First Aid box and aprons, or repair, such as the climbing frame. Planning in this way avoids the likelihood of staff complaining half-way through the year that money is not available for extra items.

The manager as an effective communicator

Developing positive and effective interpersonal relationships is one of the keys to management success. This means that every action, communication, response and consideration is influenced by your ability to know the importance of and how to:

➤ establish and maintain positive relationships
➤ perceive the needs, concerns and personal circumstances of others
➤ develop the team so that everyone is working towards a common goal
➤ identify the different stages of group dynamics
➤ recognise and resolve conflict
➤ use effective listening skills
➤ notice, interpret and respond to non-verbal behaviour
➤ make effective use of a range of oral and written communication skills
➤ give appropriate feedback in a sensitive manner.

Without effective communication, all the activities of an organisation will fail; instructions cannot be given, information cannot be provided and there would be no contact between supervisors and staff.

The early years sector is a people-intensive service, therefore the manager must be an expert communicator. You need to be able define communication for staff so

that there is a shared understanding. Stanton (1996) suggests that there are four general objectives that are true of all efforts to communicate:

➤ to be received
➤ to be understood
➤ to be accepted
➤ to get action.

According to Stanton, if we fail to achieve any one of these objectives, then it is almost conclusive that we have failed to communicate.

Communication is of course a two-way process. As well as oral and written communication, listening, body language, gesture, eye contact and tone of voice all play a significant part when we transmit messages to each other. Remember that only 7 per cent of communication is verbal, the remaining 93 per cent being non-verbal. This is a very powerful message to people with a lead responsibility for communicating and supporting others to communicate.

What are communication skills?
The ability to:

➤ listen actively
➤ ask questions
➤ check out and clarify mutual understanding
➤ identify the information needs of listeners
➤ use different communication styles appropriate to listeners and situations
➤ maintain the interest of the listener
➤ reinforce points
➤ confirm listeners' understanding, through questioning and interpretation of non-verbal signs
➤ modify communication in response to feedback from others.

Within an early years setting, there are many obstacles to be overcome in order to communicate effectively. For example:

➤ the setting is busy and noisy
➤ the needs of the children mean that staff are engaged in different and separate activities throughout the day
➤ staff may work shifts, so there is no shared time
➤ managers may have to respond to immediate demands and have no time to share the information with their team or may simply forget to do so.

These problems can cause difficulties among team members. No matter what the demands in your settings are, it is worth making sure that the team come together as a group regularly and that you have strategies in place to disseminate information and keep all lines of communication open.

Your staff also need to understand that they have a responsibility to ask questions, share information and check what is happening. Aim to reduce the number of times that you hear your staff say, 'I didn't know, no one told me'.

Manager's tip
Share information with your staff by using:
➤ notice-boards
➤ diaries
➤ 'Post-it' notes
➤ staff personal mail boxes
➤ e-mail
➤ tick lists on a chart.

Developing skills
If a manager is not able to articulate or write clearly, they will be at a significant disadvantage when attempting to deliver crucial information. It can be a serious hindrance if the author of an important communiqué is unable to convey it accurately. External agencies may request information, such as for special needs reports, children's transition to school reports and so on, where it is vital that reports be clear, accurate and presentable. Similarly nursery staff make decisions based on the

information presented to them by outside agencies. Therefore it is essential that this information be correct as it determines the strategies that are to be employed.

In order for views and opinions to be aired openly, it is imperative that you understand how to create a climate that supports and copes with free expression. It is not uncommon to hear staff say, 'You couldn't talk about that, because the manager would get really cross with you' or 'I am not telling her that, she will sulk or tell me off at the staff meeting'. If the manager is representing the staff view at other management meetings, he or she has to be able to fairly represent all the views of the staff, not just a doctored view that fits with the outcome that he or she wants. It is of equal importance that information cascading downwards be shared positively and objectively, to ensure that all staff remain committed and informed.

Increasingly we rely on the power of technological communication, but while e-mails can be helpful, they can also be quite tyrannous. Now managers not only have to respond to a list of phone calls, they also have to answer e-mails! There is

often a sense that e-mails have to be dealt with immediately; instead, aim to have two sessions a day when you check your inbox.

If you intend to maintain a database on the computer, you will need to keep the information up to date and be aware of the Data Protection Act whenever you circulate confidential material. You will need to provide guidance to staff about using any systems, including the computer and fax machines. If your staff have access to the Internet, you will need to decide on a policy for using it for personal use.

In order for any team to function effectively, communication must be a priority. The bottom line is clear – failure to communicate well will have a direct impact on the quality of care given to the children. It is easy to see the consequences of a member of staff failing to tell a colleague that a child is allergic to nuts or needs to use an inhaler. The destabilising effects of individuals who do not carry out tasks due to unclear instructions are less obvious, but have a serious undermining effect on the ability of the team to operate cohesively. It is therefore essential that managers nurture and support their staff, respecting them as individuals as well as team members. An individual who feels valued and supported will communicate that same sense of value and support not only to their colleagues but also to the children in their care.

The manager as a team builder

The staff team is the most important resource in any early years setting. In order for the manager to function effectively, it is essential that the staff team work together. A manager needs to have a vision that is shared and supported by the team so that everyone is working to the same end. It is helpful to agree on core principles that underpin the function of the organisation so that everyone knows what they are aiming for and the expectations and standards of practice that underpin these aims. However, as a manager, you also need to be able to recognise individual staff members' methods of working and their differing capabilities. This will enable you to identify their strengths and weaknesses and learn their working styles so that you can meet their individual needs. The photocopiable sheet 'Developing staff as individuals' on page 137 will help you to ensure that you are developing individual staff to their full potential.

You need to ensure that staff are kept informed, and one way of doing this is by holding regular meetings. Managers must make sure that their staff feel that their opinions are valued, and must show confidence in the team's ability to reach their targets, making each team member feel appreciated. Staff need to know that their efforts make a difference to achieving common goals.

Recognise all contributions, however small, to make staff feel valued. Celebrate your team and do not wait for a reason to praise your staff. Remember to:

➤ take the team out
➤ provide nice treats at staff meetings
➤ have a compliments book
➤ give your staff well-planned supervision.

Consider an appraisal system as a way of consolidating your staff's strengths and weaknesses, and planning how to support and develop them in these and new areas. Properly managed appraisals are a good way of valuing the individual (see Chapter 2).

Manager's tip
Use the photocopiable sheet 'Building and maintaining the team' on page 138 to check your team-building skills.

The manager as a motivator

It is important for a manager to develop a trusting relationship with all members of the team. Successful teams will thrive on mutual trust, so it is vital to establish this early on by delegation, open conduct and communication, and a free exchange of ideas. It is essential that all team members be aware of their own personal values so that they can deal effectively and objectively with situations as they arise. As the manager, you will determine the ethos of the setting and will often influence the attitudes of your staff.

Motivation, delegation and development are key features of managing a team. According to Heller (1998), people are capable of remarkable achievements if they are given the right motivational leadership. Adair (1997) shares this idea, arguing that every manager needs to be able to motivate or draw out the best from others. Huczynski and Buchanan (2000) say that different people are motivated by different outcomes, which means that an effective manager will need to be able to recognise the needs of individual team members and then provide appropriate training and support for each of them, in order to realise the whole team's potential. Successful managers will also have to be able to acknowledge and celebrate the contributions made by individual staff members in order to create a high-performing, cohesive team.

In order to motivate the team on a daily basis to achieve their jobs efficiently, as a manager you must use your influencing and negotiation skills to show your staff:

➤ the impact that they have on others by their action or example (going sick at short notice or regularly)
➤ the importance of getting involved in the process of management (having duty-manager systems)
➤ the importance of balancing individual needs with institutional requirements (staying late sometimes)
➤ the benefit of getting opinions about change in order to obtain agreement (about a work-practice issue, change to a rota, attending training).

To motivate all your staff, you will need to find ways of developing each of them. This can be achieved by offering training, coaching and development. Make sure that systems are in place to support your staff by, for example, giving someone a relatively small task to start with and building up to something more complex, offering plenty of encouragement. Give your staff different roles and responsibilities so that they can extend their knowledge and build their confidence. This will only work if the targets set are achievable and there are suitable support structures and resources available. Always encourage your staff to use their own initiative and to take ownership of their decisions. It is important that you delegate appropriately in order to give your staff opportunities to develop and to have a sense of achievement.

A manager leads by example and, according to Heller (1998), a great deal can be learned from others whose behaviour appears to get results. This is quite a responsibility for a manager, and to do this you must have an in-depth knowledge of your own role. This requires you to continually develop yourself, taking responsibility for your errors and sharing responsibility for mistakes with staff, analysing them so that they can be prevented next time. Within the context of acting as a role model, it is important that you show flexibility in a positive way, especially when dealing with change (see Chapter 4). Change is vital for success and helps organisations to grow. It helps to question established ideas or practices and develop and extend

knowledge. A great deal of change has occurred recently in early years education and the planning for and implementation of change is one of the major challenges for today's leaders in early childhood.

The manager as a decision-maker

Decision-making can be a painful process as it involves change and conflict, and the risk of being wrong and called to account. Some people will avoid making a decision on this basis, but managers cannot afford to avoid making decisions because their staff will become frustrated and sometimes virtually paralysed by the lack of decision.

Making a decision

➤ Define the situation (problems and opportunities).
➤ Establish criteria (essential or desirable).
➤ Generate alternatives.
➤ Evaluate and test the options.
➤ Select the decision.

Having gone through this process, you have to be ready to implement the decision. Some managers are sufficiently foolish or immodest to believe that whatever they have decided will be automatically done. You need to put in a checking system to ensure that the decision has been implemented consistently, not just when you are present or visible. Do this by:

➤ determining who will do what and by when (action plan)
➤ communicating the action plan with all parties concerned
➤ establishing and communicating a review procedure
➤ ensuring that reviews take place
➤ agreeing on an action plan including checking to see if everyone has really understood the contents of the decision.

There are different styles of decision-making and they are categorised in the following way:

➤ **Autocratic**: a decision is taken without consultation, then others are informed of what is to be done and what is expected of them.
➤ **Persuasive**: the decision is taken before consultation and then 'sold' to the others.
➤ **Consultative**: the views of others are sought and taken into account before the decision is taken.
➤ **Consensus**: decisions are taken on a majority basis.

The appropriate style for decision-making will depend on the people and circumstances, and effective decisions depend on commitment. While all staff like to be involved in decision-making, there is overwhelming evidence that most people would like a greater share than they have in the decisions that affect them but that are the responsibility of others.

The role of the manager as teacher

The job of every manager is to help other people to be successful by creating conditions where it is likely that people will succeed because they are able, willing and supported. The best way to do this is to focus on creating and managing an environment where achieving and learning are complementary activities. Do this by:

➤ creating an environment where learning is built into conversation, meetings and supervision

➤ clarifying what people have learned, for example, at the end of a meeting, ask people one thing that they have learned from the meeting and one thing that they will implement and why

➤ making the link between what has been learned and improved performance

➤ creating an environment where continuous learning is seen as a process of self-development and where learning is always on the agenda.

The manager as supervisor

Early years managers have a crucial supervisory role because it is their responsibility to ensure the smooth running of the setting. It is essential that they be aware of their own personal values so that they can deal effectively and objectively with situations as they arise. As a manager, you will determine the ethos of the setting and often influence the attitudes of people working for you.

As an early years manager, you need to have a clear understanding of personal boundaries between the people working in the team. While you are aiming to create a happy, friendly, caring environment, this must not lead to compromising friendships between yourself and the team. It is essential that your staff have a clear understanding of your role as manager and do not misinterpret their relationship with you. For example, if they perceive you as a 'friend', there is a danger that they will not accept your criticism as a manager. You will need to be aware of the group dynamics in order to maintain standards and continue working towards shared goals.

It is essential that the manager be a self-reflective practitioner who understands the complexities of the role and operates in a non-discriminatory manner, enabling and empowering their staff team. Facilitating feedback sessions, holding staff meetings and creating a culture of openness act as safeguards against bias, as does adherence to employment law, health and safety guidelines, and equal opportunities policies. Working within an infrastructure that includes clear guidelines on policies and procedures, along with job descriptions and person specifications, all help to sustain the manager's professionalism.

Often the most personally difficult aspect of the supervisory role is that it is inevitable at some point that you will be unpopular with your staff. Maintaining standards, setting targets, introducing change, managing conflict, conducting appraisals and implementing grievance and disciplinary procedures, all contribute towards the staff's view of their manager – and this may not be a positive one! It is essential that as an early years manager you remain focused on your role as facilitator and leader, and you must not lose sight of your priority – the care and education of the children in your setting. The weak manager who compromises on standards in order to remain popular, or capitulates at the first sign of resistance, is harming both their subordinates and the organisation. Not only are they reducing

Manager's tip
Good managers have the ability to:
➤ generate enthusiasm and energy
➤ give a clear sense of direction
➤ combine vision with practical application
➤ be clear about the needs and goals of the organisation
➤ mix knowledge, skills, personal attitudes and values to the best effect
➤ make decisions
➤ harness the staff's energy and enthusiasm to develop the setting
➤ encourage initiative and risk-taking, and have tolerance of failure
➤ develop a management style that empowers people to do their job without abdicating accountability.

the quality of service but they are also neglecting their role as mentor and enabler. On the other hand, the firm manager who acts fairly is likely to gain respect and be successful.

Use the photocopiable sheets 'Managing every day in the setting' on pages 139–141 as a useful way of looking at your overall management skills.

NVQ in Management Level 3

The NVQ in Management Level 3 has been designed to meet the needs of practising managers with specific and defined responsibility, including managing staff, activities, budgets, resources and information.

The Award is based on five levels, reflecting the complexity, responsibility and autonomy of the job. Candidates must provide evidence that they consistently perform at this level and show that they have the underpinning knowledge and understanding to show that they can use their skills and abilities to perform in other contexts and circumstances.

The NVQ Standards are built on competencies, which are sets of statements that describe what a staff member is required to do within their job role. The key features of competencies are that they are based on explicit statements of performance and related underpinning knowledge, assessed on actual performance, together with application of relevant knowledge.

Candidates completing the NVQ in Management Level 3 have to complete five mandatory units and two optional units from a choice of eight. It is important that candidates choose units that are activities which are part of their daily work. The mandatory units are:

A1   Maintain activities to meet requirements
B1   Support the efficient use of resources
C1   Manage yourself
C4   Create effective working relationships
D1   Manage information for action.

Each unit is made up of performance criteria that candidates have to demonstrate that they can carry out within the work place, and this is underpinned by 'knowledge requirements', which are the theory and guidance that candidates have to apply to their performance. In addition, candidates have to show that they can perform in a range of contexts and situations – these are the 'evidence requirements'.

Each chapter throughout this book ends with a section called 'NVQ in Management Level 3 links'. This section links the relevant performance criteria and knowledge requirements to the chapter – for example, 'Managing finance' (Chapter 7) is linked to the evidence that candidates would need to show for Unit B1. In addition, a candidate completing the NVQ in Management Level 3 needs to demonstrate personal competencies for each unit. These are identified on the photocopiable sheets 'NVQ in Management Level 3 links' on pages 142 and 143, and are designed to help managers to decide if they can collect the relevant evidence in their current job.

Case study

Below is a case study that could be used as a staff-meeting discussion point. Talk about what you would do and why.

You have recently taken over the management of a large team. The staff group is a diverse group and there is some loyalty to the previous manager who was a 'larger than life' character and who had her own ways of doing things. The general impression that you have is of a group who will do what they are told when given a task but show no initiative, who tend to arrive and leave promptly, even if tasks are left unfinished, and have no real enthusiasm. More importantly, you are concerned that the team are functioning as a group of individuals rather than as a whole team.

Consider what you would do with regards to:

➤ the atmosphere of the group, which is negative and lukewarm, and the impact that this could have on the parents, carers and children

➤ identifying the symptoms of low morale, such as a weakening of resolve and a loss of a sense of purpose and signs of mistrust, as well as decline in professional and personal standards

➤ checking if the staff group lost its sense of direction

➤ finding out whether each individual member is still clear about the team's principal aim

➤ whether all groups have potential 'metal fatigue' cracks and checking if these cracks are widening into divisions between individuals, cliques or subgroups

➤ finding out which individuals are underachieving when measured against the setting standards

➤ potential staff complaints.

Useful information

➤ The Chartered Management Institute, Management House, Cottingham Road, Corby, Northamptonshire NN17 1TT. Tel: 01536-204 222. Also 2 Savoy Court, Strand, London WC2R 0EZ. Tel: 020-7497 0580. Website: www.inst-mgt.org.uk

➤ Chartered Institute of Personnel and Development (CIPD), CIPD House, Camp Road, Wimbledon, London SW19 4UX. Tel: 020-8971 9000. Website: www.cipd.co.uk

➤ The Council for Awards in Children's Care and Education, 8 Chequer Street, St Albans, Hertfordshire AL1 3XZ. Tel: 01727-847 636. Website: www.cache.org.uk

➤ ChildcareLink, tel: 0800-096 0296, website: www.childcarelink.org.uk The ChildcareLink service was launched by the Government in December 1999 as part of the National Childcare Strategy.

Chapter 2 Supporting and developing staff

- ➤ **Recruitment and selection**
- ➤ **Developing a recruitment strategy**
- ➤ **Staff induction**
- ➤ **Understanding your staff**
- ➤ **Creating a motivating environment**
- ➤ **Planning a training programme**
- ➤ **Becoming a coaching manager**
- ➤ **Providing information for staff**
- ➤ **Supervising and appraising staff**
- ➤ **Dealing with under-performance**

One of the manager's responsibilities is to support and develop their staff so that they can do their jobs well. This is a significant task and one never to be underestimated, and it is particularly crucial in a people-intensive area such as early years. Supporting staff is a very effective means of retaining staff, which is particularly important in today's climate, given the significant staff shortages across all early years settings.

Studies among staff in all sectors have found that they valued training and development opportunities more than financial benefits. The Hay Group asked one million staff members, from a range of different sectors, to identify the most significant factor that kept them with their current employer: 83 per cent said that it was the opportunity to use skills and abilities, and 66 per cent said that it was the ability to learn new skills.

An early years setting is only as good as the staff working there. Parents will recognise this and will look for a stable staff group who are informed, knowledgeable and motivated. Children know it because they have interested staff who provide a stimulating and lively environment for them. Staff know when they are valued and encouraged to learn and share their learning, where they are motivated by appropriate challenges and opportunities that keep them alert, enthusiastic and excited to come to work.

The development of people is not additional to a service but at the very heart of performance. Without effective people, the setting will fail. Some managers may wonder why they need to put so much effort into staff development when staff may leave and take all the support and training that were given to them to another setting. However, it is best to have a well-developed team when they are with you, rather than a mediocre group of staff who stay forever. To remain on top, your setting must make best use of all the staff, developing their potential and recognising and utilising their talents. The outcome will be that you are managing a high-performance staff team, and benefiting from being part of an effective and emotionally in-tune setting.

Recruitment and selection

Advertising vacancies

Attracting, recruiting and developing staff is key to the success of any setting. The skill in recruiting successfully is to select the right people and make them want to join you. In a competitive market, advertising is very important.

Ensure that your job advertisement includes all the necessary information about salary, skills, qualifications, role, hours of work and benefits (see below).

Would you like to share in the success of a thriving children's centre?
If so, this may be the job for you.

Nursery Officer
Salary: (*add salary details*)

Poppy Lane is a drop-in centre in East London, which supports children, their families and carers of pre-school children. We recently received a very successful OFSTED inspection report, which recognised the impact that we have on the local community. We are looking for an experienced nursery officer to join our small friendly team.

You will need to be qualified with NNEB, DNN, BTEC, NVQ 3 or equivalent, with at least two years' experience of working in a group care setting.

An ability to work within a team, provide sensitive and stimulating activities for children, write and implement children's care plans, assess children's progress and contribute to a healthy and safe environment are essential.

The vacant post is for 37 hours per week and there is some flexibility in the hours. Our benefit package includes pension scheme, family-friendly policies and ongoing training and development.

    Closing date: (*add date*)

    Interview date: (*add date*)

    For an application pack, please contact (*add contact details*)

    CVs will not be considered.

➤ Consider where you advertise. Use relevant sources and publications and keep a record of how many applicants applied from each source.

➤ Develop a marketing strategy for filling childcare places as well as attracting staff. Let everyone hear good things about the setting. Get in the habit of sending articles about your events, achievements and anything of interest to local papers and national childcare publications. Invite the local press to events.

➤ Build yourself a good reputation. In early years, word of mouth is very powerful; the majority of childcare vacancies are filled in this way. Parents and carers, potential staff, students, funders, inspectors and support agencies will all be influenced by the information that they get about your setting. Reading a poor report on the Internet or hearing negative comments from colleagues will be enough to deter potential staff.

➤ Put together a good recruitment pack. This needs to include:
  - information about the setting
  - where it is
  - type of staff and their roles

- job descriptions
- details of staff training
- links with other professionals and agencies.

The information needs to be useful and stimulating to encourage people to want to join. If you can afford it, produce a colour brochure about your group.

➤ Constantly check why staff want to join your setting and what makes them stay. Ask interviewees what attracted them to the job advert. Carry out a regular internal questionnaire asking staff:

- why they like working for the setting
- what improvements would make life better
- what makes them feel valued
- how you can improve the service for new staff
- if they would encourage their friends to join the setting and why.

Developing a recruitment strategy

Consider how to make recruitment part of your setting's staff training and development, as a means of ensuring that succession planning is high on the agenda. This is particularly crucial for ensuring that important roles are likely to be filled, so that there is no significant gap when the post holder leaves.

➤ Have training and coaching programmes to prepare and develop staff for internal promotions and qualifications.

➤ Advertising, application forms, the taking-up of references, shortlisting and interviews should all take account of the principles of data protection and the code of practice on recruitment and selection published in March 2002. For example, collect only personal information relevant to the job, be careful how you use and share it, ensure that candidates understand why and which information will be collected and how it will be used, and establish a policy on keeping recruitment records.

➤ Think about how students and agency staff may become future staff.

➤ Provide training for volunteers and parents or carers who may become future staff.

➤ Make a database of local colleges, training centres and job agencies, and send them copies of your brochure. Link into the Early Years Development and Childcare Partnership, which also collects and disseminates this information.

➤ Hold an open evening for local students.

➤ Attend local and national job fairs.

➤ Consider ways of attracting staff to your area, especially if you are based in expensive areas. Provide information on accessible and affordable housing.

➤ Offer advice on interviewing techniques to internal staff to help them compete with external candidates, when they seek internal promotion.

➤ Consider having available supply staff, such as special needs assistants.

➤ Retaining staff essentially requires listening to the needs of individual employees and responding creatively by offering flexible working hours, attracting older staff or giving unpaid time to help cope with domestic crises.

Information for the staff member

Write a comprehensive job description that clearly defines the role of the staff member. This is very important because it will tell the staff member and the manager what they have to do as a requirement of the job. It will also define the skills required to do the job. Refer to the photocopiable sheet 'Nursery Officer job description' on page 144 for a sample job description for the role of nursery officer.

A job description needs:

➤ a title – this should reflect the post as accurately as possible.
➤ the purpose of the job – a short paragraph outlining the general objective of the post. This may begin with 'To create', 'To develop' or 'To provide'.
➤ a person specification – the skills, experience and attitude needed.
➤ tasks or duties – a list of the different elements of the job. Aim to list between ten and 15; any more and the job tasks are either too specific or too numerous. Use subheadings such as 'Health and safety' and 'Team participation'.

Before embarking on a round of recruitment, check that the job description is still valid. Use the job description as a basis for a development plan and appraisal. A job description is not just a document that comes with the information pack when a staff member begins a new job – it is a useful tool.

When people respond to adverts, give them a prompt reply. If they are invited for interview, be warm and welcoming and make sure that all other staff are, too. If you reject them, be fair and professional.

The interview

The interview should be structured and aim to give you the information that you need to make an appointment. Agree who will conduct the interviews, according to the post required. Inviting existing staff to appear on an interviewing panel is a very positive way to develop their own skills. Run a regular selection and recruitment course and give all staff the opportunity to attend, not just senior staff. Attending an interviewing panel can open staff members' eyes to the complexity of finding new staff and will probably reduce comments such as, 'Why did they employ her, she's useless' when they themselves have been on an interviewing panel.

Draft the interview questions against the requirements of the job description and person specification. Devise a form on which each of the criteria is recorded (see the photocopiable sheets 'Person specification for a nursery officer' on pages 145 and 146). At the end of the interview, record your judgement on the form to indicate whether you thought that the candidate gave sufficient evidence to meet each of the criteria. The panel as a whole can then go through all the comments and agree on a final decision against the same set of criteria for each candidate.

Ensure that the interview is conducted in a quiet, well-ventilated room. Offer candidates a drink and provide glasses of water. Throughout the interview be firm but polite and friendly. Remember that an interview is a two-way process. An interviewing panel that undermines candidates is not likely to encourage them to want to join your setting, nor is it likely to bring out the best in them.

At the end of the interview, check contact details and give a clear indicator of when and how you will be in touch. When you are, give clear reasons for deciding whether or not they meet the criteria. Make an offer to the candidate as soon as possible, by telephone later that day if you can. For unsuccessful candidates, emphasise that they were unsuitable for the job, not unsuitable as people. Be kind in your rejection letter and, if possible, offer them the opportunity for feedback.

Once the person is appointed, you need to ensure that they know their employment rights. This includes knowledge of salary details, of personnel policies, of what information is kept on their personal file, access to this information, training support and conditions of work in your setting. Remember that all staff must have a contract of employment.

Information summary

The contract of employment should include:

➤ employer's name
➤ employee's name
➤ date employment began
➤ amount of pay and the frequency of payment (monthly or weekly)
➤ hours of work
➤ holiday pay and entitlement.

The main personnel policies are:

➤ recruitment and selection policy
➤ disciplinary policy
➤ maternity leave policy
➤ special leave policy
➤ grievance policy
➤ induction policy
➤ probation policy
➤ overtime or TOIL (time off in lieu) policies
➤ staff development policy.

Personnel files might contain:

➤ personal details: name, gender, date of birth, address, education, qualifications, previous experience, tax code, National Insurance number, next of kin, details of any disability
➤ employment details: date employment began, date present job started, job title, basic pay, overtime or other pay premiums
➤ absence details: sickness, lateness, special leave, special requests regarding leave, annual leave quota (authorised and unauthorised)
➤ details of any accidents at work
➤ details of disciplinary action
➤ training details.

Get the recruitment process right; this is very important because if it is done badly it can lead to:

➤ poor performance
➤ unnecessary training
➤ increased supervision
➤ wasted management time
➤ high staff turnover
➤ higher absence
➤ low morale.

Remember: it is important to try to anticipate employment needs not just for next month, but for the next year and further ahead. Use succession planning as a tool to guide the management of the setting.

Staff induction

When a new staff member joins, go out of your way to make their first day a happy one. One of the worst things that you can do is to throw a new recruit in at the deep end, while everyone watches them either sink or swim. Instead, give them a clear message that new people are valued and welcome. Treating newcomers well also gives positive messages to existing staff.

If your setting is large, you may consider inviting new staff to spend a couple of hours in the head office getting to know all the key staff there. You could also arrange a meeting with the personnel officer to go through their employment details and clarify any confusion or answer queries.

Plan the induction

Prepare to receive your new recruit into the work place. Plan their induction and basic training and put in a checking system so that you know that it has been completed properly. Allocate this task to a staff member who can coach them or who has managed students previously. Again, this is a useful learning opportunity for existing staff. Sometimes it is a good task to give a recently appointed, confident

staff member who may empathise with the new staff member, recognise their worries and fears, while also giving them an opportunity to reinforce their own grasp of your setting's policies and procedures.

Pace the induction process to take account of the new staff member's previous experience, their learning approach, the size of your setting, the demands of the children and the time of year they have joined. For example, if they join the setting near Christmas, they may find themselves in a whirl of social events that may mean the induction is slightly more convoluted. During the first few days, focus on basic issues such as:

➤ the layout of the building
➤ location of fire exits and key health and safety features of the building
➤ times of the shifts
➤ names of colleagues
➤ simple daily routine
➤ staff room and arrangements for meals and drinks, for example, whether they will eat with the children or bring sandwiches, if they need to provide a personal mug and where to find the nearest sandwich shop.

Remember the little foibles of each setting that are taken for granted by existing staff but could be a real barrier to new staff, such as who uses which cup and where people sit. Allocate the new staff member a 'buddy' to look after them for the first few days. Make sure that you complete the induction process and build in regular check-in times to confirm the person's grasp of the process.

As soon as staff members settle into the team, continue to treat them well. People can be insecure for a lot longer then you realise and for many people the first six months in a new job will be daunting. No matter how busy you are, make time to ask how new staff are settling in, and remember little personal details, such as asking how their own child has coped with a recent exam and so on. Your staff will be genuinely pleased to receive this personal and friendly approach from you.

Have a probation meeting

Many settings have a six-month probation period for new staff. At the end of this time a probation meeting is used to confirm their appointment. It is not an opportunity to raise major concerns about the person's practice; if there are concerns about the new staff member's competence, it should have been raised with them before this time.

At the probation meeting it is useful to go through the person's job description, picking out areas for further development. Let them lead the process, commenting and giving their view of their first six months in their new setting – they may identify areas for improvement themselves. Agree on a six-month action plan that can then be worked through in regular supervision meetings (see the sample probation form on the photocopiable sheets 'Probation form for nursery staff' on pages 147–149).

Understanding your staff

Management is about understanding, developing and motivating people. Development and motivation are inextricably linked. Good managers need to understand themselves and others and, most importantly, their attitudes to their staff. Staff will not commit to an uncommitted manager, so it is important that you motivate yourself as well as others. Managers need to get to know why people behave as they do in order to understand their needs.

Work places are often very emotional places and people can behave in a very self-protective way. They can respond with very powerful reactions to what seem to be the most benign of requests. They can be defensive and aggressive about the most minor change or criticism and might leap to unsubstantiated conclusions, gather into cliques and gang up on one another. Their responses can baffle even the most experienced managers.

It often feels much easier to work with the children than understand how the staff think, respond and reach conclusions! However, as a manager, you must remain fair and objective. If you react in the same way as the staff, there is real cause for concern. You may feel like throwing your hands up in horror and telling them all to 'grow up', but that would probably do more harm than good (although you may feel very invigorated at the time!). Such behaviour may mask the staff's real fears or insecurity. You must find out what is happening and respond appropriately. You have to understand that your response will either motivate and support or demotivate and alienate your staff. It is much harder to move on from the latter position.

The Institute of Manpower conducted a survey to find out why staff left their settings. The majority said that they were leaving their managers rather than their settings. They said that instead of giving fair and supportive feedback, their managers were inconsistent, unapproachable, inclined to favouritism and unwilling to consult. This report thus highlights the important role that managers play in retaining staff.

Treat staff well and motivate them

'Treat other people as you would like to be treated' is a good motto to have pinned on the staff notice-board. Managers need to remember this and consider how they treat their staff. A committed, motivated staff member is extremely valuable and each early years setting is as good as the staff working there. You must recognise this and make every effort to gain staff commitment.

Maslow (1943), in identifying his hierarchy of needs, argued that people are motivated by their strongest need at any point in time. Managers need to first provide for people's key needs, and then they need to look at how they are going to support staff towards self-actualisation, where they reach a point of positive self-motivation. Imagine the joy of managing staff who want to learn, who have sorted out the routine without a murmur, who have developed new initiatives and tested them to benefit the service, who are supportive, keen and interested and who buoy each other up on a wave of enthusiasm and interest. You can go a long way to enable your staff to reach this stage if you:

➤ continually encourage them to make suggestions for efficiency improvements, prompting a sense of involvement in a task and a commitment to its success
➤ create a blame-free, learning, 'can do' culture
➤ ensure that each employee has a stimulating variety of tasks to perform
➤ demonstrate loyalty to the staff team
➤ pay attention to people at all levels
➤ provide the resources and training through which new skills can be developed
➤ raise interest levels
➤ review staff opportunities to avoid boredom through repetition
➤ tolerate individuality
➤ trust others and be trusted to do what you say you will.

According to Herzberg, as mentioned in Fearns (2001), a manager should provide motivators that will encourage people to want to achieve. Staff should be given responsibilities that enrich their jobs, as well as opportunities for self-advancement, and managers should make sure that when they allocate more responsibility to their staff, it is a two-way process and that the staff members do not feel put upon.

The level of responsibility given also has to be considered carefully. It is inappropriate to ask a member of staff to take on a more responsible job if they are not allowed to make the appropriate decisions associated with the post. If you really want to enrich someone's job, it has to be done so that the whole team sees it as a new and exciting opportunity. This will give everyone a positive message, that all staff are valued and that everyone will have development opportunities.

Any new task is a development opportunity and must be treated as such. The staff member must be prepared and supported to take on the new responsibility. For example, one member of the team may be very interested in the issue of special needs; they may also be showing interest in extending their work responsibilities. You may therefore consider this person for the role of SENCO. In this case you would need to provide a proper SENCO induction, possibly led by the previous post holder – it would not be enough to simply ask the person to take on the role. In addition you could offer the person some relevant reading material, a subscription to a magazine or perhaps a training course, to help them prepare to take on the new tasks. This will then ensure that the new role becomes an enriching experience,

Manager's tip
These are the ten qualities that people want most from their jobs:
➤ to work for efficient managers
➤ to think for themselves
➤ to see the end result of their work
➤ to be assigned interesting work
➤ to be informed
➤ to be listened to
➤ to be respected
➤ to be recognised for their efforts
➤ to be challenged
➤ to have opportunities for increased skills development.

rather than a traumatising one where the member of staff fails and feels incompetent and demotivated (see the photocopiable sheets 'Induction programme for a new SENCO' on pages 162–164).

Praise and provide feedback

Acknowledging excellence is vital in maintaining a staff member's commitment and job satisfaction. Always recognise good performance formally; people need to feel that their contribution is valued and unique. Staff are often proud of their individual achievements but they are also proud of the collective effort and they like to associate with a successful team.

Praise people publicly and privately, do not just reward excellence or great achievements. Remember those members of staff who plod along consistently, ensuring that everything is done on time. Remind everyone of the importance of the domestic and routine tasks as well as the unusual, one-off jobs. Aim to give positive feedback all the time and tell your staff how well they are doing. Consider using the same model as the one that you adopt with the children: say something positive, identifying exactly what has pleased you, for example, 'That display is

fantastic, the way that you have balanced two- and three-dimensional objects is very eye-catching, thank you' or 'Thank you for the report, it was very well presented and it summed up the main points really clearly'.

Think about other ways of praising and thanking staff:

➤ Do you have a staff outing?
➤ Do you have a staff newsletter or update?
➤ Does the training department produce a newsletter that includes information about the staff?
➤ Do you take the staff out for a drink or a meal occasionally?
➤ Do you encourage the team to go out to celebrate surviving a busy term?
➤ Do you buy nice biscuits for the meetings?
➤ Do you consider other perks that show people when they are valued?
➤ Do you have an award ceremony for staff that are completing awards?

Consider everything that you do which values your staff, make sure that you give them a positive message and never underestimate the value of a simple 'thank you'.

Creating a motivating environment

The role of the manager in training and staff development is to create an environment with a culture of learning, so that staff feel continually challenged and are never bored. They should:

➤ have a willingness and an appetite for learning
➤ be able to cope with change and reach new challenges
➤ be innovative and able to use their learning to problem-solve and innovate.

In order to be successful as a manager, you need to understand how to create a 'can do' supportive environment, where there is a free exchange of information and ideas. You need to be able to create an atmosphere of mutual trust that is underpinned by the shared belief that everyone is continuously learning, throughout every aspect of the setting.

➤ Develop a clear vision for your setting, ensuring that all the staff know and understand it.

➤ Help the staff to make the link between the aims of your setting, their individual performance and development planning. Make sure that they understand how they fit into the overall plan. For example, if the aim of your setting is to increase the health and safety profile, help your staff to see why they have to do COSHH (Control of Substances Hazardous to Health) training or to contribute to risk assessments, even though they feel that this reduces their quality time with the children.

➤ Value training and development as the key to the development of staff and the setting. These elements are often highly prized when everything is going well, but at the first sign of trouble the training budget is cut, just when it is needed to motivate the staff to cope with the consequences of difficult times.

➤ Recognise that learning is continuous and that it needs to be apparent throughout your setting.

➤ Have subscriptions to weekly and monthly magazines and provide a set of useful up-to-date reference books for your staff to use.

➤ Use key staff development policies and procedures, including supervision, appraisals and job recruitment, to make a positive difference to all staff.

➤ Encourage your staff to manage their own learning – this is also an effective way of spreading learning around your setting.

➤ Develop your own learning and let the staff know that you are doing this.

➤ Have a system to check that learning opportunities are available to all staff; some staff will avoid engaging in any activity and others may want to do everything.

➤ Consider a system of checking each staff member's learning style so that there is a balance of methods available to meet everyone's needs comfortably.

➤ Make coaching key to your service. Honey and Mumford (1982) describe managers as possible trendsetters, who create an environment where the emphasis is on continuous development. In order to help this process, they identify ten ways that we can increase learning and ten traits of the opposite behaviour, which decreases learning.

Behaviour that increases learning
➤ asking questions
➤ suggesting ideas
➤ exploring options
➤ taking risks or experimenting
➤ being open
➤ admitting inadequacies and mistakes
➤ converting mistakes into learning opportunities
➤ reflecting and reviewing
➤ discussing what has been learned
➤ taking responsibility for own learning.

Behaviour that decreases learning

➤ acquiescing
➤ putting people's ideas down
➤ going for expedient quick fixes
➤ being cautious
➤ telling people what they want to hear
➤ justifying actions and/or blaming other people or events
➤ repeating the same mistakes
➤ rushing around keeping active
➤ discussing what happened without 'lessons learned' and plans to improve
➤ waiting for other people to do things.

Encourage your staff to understand that learning is not a quick fix. It cannot be covered by a two-day course but has to be part of a long-term programme. Introduce annual development planning for each team. Invite them to look at no more than four targets for the year and link some of those to your setting targets. For example, the setting may be focusing on developing health and safety and the team may decide that this is a good time for them to advance some of their own training skills. However, they also may want to improve the science area of the setting and may be considering improving how they use the outdoor area. Use a format that enables the staff to consider the financial costs associated with their plans, and introduce the concept of the **SMART** (**S**pecific **M**easurable **A**ttainable **R**ealistic **T**ime-bound) target.

Develop a form on which to log your setting's agreed targets by writing the following questions:

1 What steps need to be taken to complete the target?
2 Who will do what?
3 What help will be needed?
4 What financial assistance will be needed and where will you get it?
5 What are the management checking systems, so that you know that the allocated staff are completing their set tasks?
6 Where will you display the development plan, so it is always in the forefront of staff thinking?
7 How will you know when you have met the targets?
8 How and when will you share this information, and with whom?

Managers need to develop the confidence to create an environment where asking questions and checking understanding is part of the culture. For example, every time you discuss problems with staff, ask questions such as, 'Why do you think that happened?', 'Are you familiar with that policy?' and 'What policy would you use to sort this out and why?'. In this way you will be encouraging them to develop new skills and knowledge. When there are mistakes made, accept the failures as an indicator that the bigger picture needs to be reviewed. Never respond by saying, 'Well, I told her how to do it'; instead, consider why the failure has occurred.

Prepare your staff for promotion and create an environment where people feel comfortable about identifying their future interests. However, do not let anyone assume that they can fit straight into the next job. Make it clear that the needs of the setting are constantly changing and that you will need people with the right balance of skills and knowledge. Remind staff that ambition is good but it has to be backed up with abilities, skills and experience.

Finally, a positive learning environment is one where there is plenty of evaluation and reflection. As a manager, you will need to put in place adequate checking systems to ensure that learning is being assimilated and cascaded down to other staff members.

Planning a training programme

Use your annual staff training and development appraisal to influence the kind of training that you plan for the year ahead. This ensures a cost-effective approach to planning training. Take account of the setting's development targets, which will be influenced by external requirements, including legal changes such as the introduction of the Care Standards, the Foundation Stage and the expansion of ICT. In addition, staff will need core training to be updated in areas such as child protection, paediatric first aid and manual handling, as well as opportunities for further development in new areas.

When you provide a programme of training for staff, publish a comprehensive plan in advance and make sure that all staff have access to the programme. Some settings have their own education facilities and many engage outside trainers and advisers. External training, in whatever form, is very costly, and managers need to be very clear about why and how they will use it effectively.

You may find that some staff want to go on every course and others avoid ever attending any training. Explore this behaviour, which indicates a need for a more strategic approach to your training provision. Staff need to be encouraged to constantly improve their range of skills, but they also need to be sensible and thoughtful about why and how they will use these new skills and the impact that training can have both positively and negatively on the setting.

Staff sometimes say that 'the training was free', but remind them that training is never free, because they have had to be released from their posts for the training time. Explain that their absence places pressure on their colleagues and may mean that someone has to give up an opportunity to do an interesting activity or does not have time to write up their work because they are covering for their colleague. Display a record of staff attendance on training courses for all to see (use the photocopiable sheet 'Record of staff attendance on training courses' on page 150).

Barriers to training
Acknowledge the barriers to training:

➤ time
➤ staff absences
➤ limited training budget
➤ conflicting priorities
➤ rigid structures
➤ failure to identify need until it is too late and the opportunities are unavailable
➤ lack of staff training and development planning.

Share with staff these barriers so that they can take some responsibilities for dealing with them. If they know that being absent from work will mean someone cannot attend the child protection course, which then means there is a shortage of that expertise in the team, they may reconsider whether they make the extra effort and come to work. If the training budget is limited, staff can research other sources of funding through the Early Years Development and Childcare Partnership, Learning Skills Council, local college bursaries and so on.

When you send staff on training course, whether internal or external, make sure that they evaluate their training experience. Use the photocopiable sheet 'After-course questionnaire' on page 151 to check whether the staff enjoyed the training or not and whether it met their original objectives. This form is unlikely to give you evidence of the impact of the training on practice, so send a learning-impact questionnaire (see the photocopiable sheet 'Learning-impact evaluation form' on page 152) to selected staff 12 weeks after they have completed their course. This will be based on the 'use it or lose it' model. In addition, talk to staff members on their return from training and ask them to do a presentation at the staff meeting to help them cascade their learning and consolidate key learning points to other staff. This is also an excellent opportunity to develop presentation skills.

Monitoring, review and evaluation process

Training is an investment in people. Its purpose is to increase staff competence, develop staff potential and improve performance. You need to collect feedback on the training programme in order to assess the value of the training and the transfer of learning. These methods of evaluation can be used to collect different information:

➤ reaction evaluation, which measures the immediate reaction of participants to the training
➤ learning evaluation, which measures the change in people's skills, knowledge, attitudes and practice
➤ performance evaluation, which measures the change in the participant's job performance over a period of time as a result of training
➤ impact performance, which looks at the effectiveness of training by assessing the type and degree of change that participants have had on the organisation or group with which they work.

All four methods will help to know:

➤ if training was effective
➤ if money was well spent
➤ if you received feedback about trainers' performance (particularly about new external trainers)
➤ if trainers received feedback about their performance and methods
➤ if learning was linked to original objectives
➤ if subsequent programmes can be improved
➤ the extent to which training objectives have been achieved and whether further training needs remain.

It is a good idea to set up a regular system which ensures that managers collect feedback and gain a sense of how the training impacts on the service.

Manager's tip
➤ Make sure that managers have training too.
➤ Keep on learning and improving.
➤ Design training courses to meet the needs of the setting.
➤ Evaluate all training.

Becoming a coaching manager

Most settings today accept that to retain good staff it is increasingly necessary to create an atmosphere of learning and growth. This calls for a manager who can:

➤ coach
➤ teach
➤ lead employees to new challenges
➤ make people feel good about themselves
➤ keep individuals motivated and interested.

Managers have a strong coaching role and you need to recognise this very powerful part of your role. Good managers are good coaches. They understand how and why they should facilitate learning and development. They know that 80 per cent of learning comes from a range of activities often termed 'informal', which include learning from colleagues, from work itself and from coaching. Indeed, they understand about learning styles and the different ways that people learn. They know how to use coaching both to help individuals to develop their full potential, and to rectify a performance deficiency in a more positive and less threatening way.

A coaching environment is one where staff are encouraged to share their learning, by reflecting on the successes and challenges of each activity. This can be in casual conversation or through a focused open question, but if carried out regularly it begins to instil a reflective attitude among staff. Mistakes can also contribute a useful learning experience, provided that the atmosphere allows for analysis, without blame or condemnation. In doing this, managers automatically start to build a more secure environment, reducing staff anxiety and encouraging a more proactive and confident staff team. This, in turn, can have a positive effect on staff, because lack of confidence often holds people back from seeking out or sometimes accepting new challenges at work. Even very confident people operate at a very small percentage of their maximum capacity or potential. Coaching each other is a safe way to develop these skills and when you suggest that staff carry out an induction programme with a new staff member, you can work through the 'I can't do that' attitude and show them how to move forward.

Managers who are coaches are recognised because they:

➤ know their staff
➤ model positive behaviour
➤ are interested in their staff
➤ look for potential in their staff
➤ help staff to think for themselves
➤ show confidence in their staff
➤ encourage responsibility
➤ maximise *ad hoc* and planned coaching opportunities
➤ never miss opportunities to coach
➤ are prepared to take risks to help their staff learn
➤ give constructive, fair and helpful feedback so that staff know what goals they have to reach and how they can be helped to get there
➤ allocate jobs that offer learning opportunities, such as leading a staff meeting or working group for a policy development, or supervising students

➤ use good questioning and listening skills

➤ make sure that staff know what is expected of them

➤ keep staff motivated and interested

➤ set priorities for the setting through the annual development plan

➤ provide new, growth experiences and challenges

➤ develop staff training and plan development programmes taking account of staff members' potential, interest and personal growth

➤ open up new horizons for everyone

➤ praise staff and recognise their work and all improvements in performance.

Providing information for staff

In early years settings, heavy emphasis is placed on the importance of communication. Yet, despite the best efforts by managers, staff can regularly be heard saying, 'I didn't know', 'No one told me' or 'I don't know where that is kept'. The message is that we can never communicate enough. That means not just giving the message but checking that the content of the message was received clearly and accurately. Invite people to feed the message back to you so that you are both clear about what was said. It is amazing how often simple messages are misunderstood. The consequences can be quite serious, for example, if information about a child's health was not communicated clearly.

Managers need to be able to communicate in order to help their staff communicate. They need to understand and read body language and identify those subtle clues that tell them much more than words. Managers need to be active listeners and be able to share information clearly and openly, both informally and formally, so that everyone understands the message, and rumours and gossip are discouraged.

Managers must respond to any requests from their staff promptly. One of the complaints about managers from staff is that they 'never return their calls', 'often lose their information in a pile of paper' or 'fail to send the relevant information requested'. This may be unfair criticism but if that is the perception you need to change it.

The days when the manager knew all the information but failed to share it with his or her staff should have ended! Now, everybody should know about everything that concerns them directly or indirectly, in full and accurate detail, as soon as possible. It is very annoying and sometimes unsafe if a deputy or other staff member cannot answer a question about the waiting-list or the budget because 'the manager does that'. Put in place a duty-manager system where all the qualified staff gradually learn how to be in charge. Everyone should know how to do everything that is part of the working day. This empowers staff and encourages them to develop and take responsibility. It puts a stop to the 'I can't do that because I don't know how' attitude.

To motivate team members, engage them in decisions that might affect them (see Chapters 4 and 5) instead of merely informing them after the fact. If people express concern about a new policy, encourage them to tell you how you can

allay their concerns. Undertake to report back on any problems that they pinpoint, and let them know how you plan to proceed, using their input. By involving staff members at an early stage, you will be encouraging them to feel that they can make a difference.

A single channel of communication is never enough: use notice-boards, communication books, internal memos, staff questionnaires and minutes from meetings. (For more details on how to communicate, refer to the section 'The manager as an effective communicator' pages 8–10.)

Staff meetings are very useful ways of supporting staff, seeking their views and checking for areas for improvement. They are also an important method of keeping people informed and provide an opportunity to answer their questions. These meetings should be conducted in a formal way and you can use them as a development opportunity. Plan well for them, reading the minutes from previous meetings, planning the agenda carefully and giving enough time for discussion. Invite staff to take turns as Chair and taking the minutes for the meetings, which is a helpful learning opportunity, if staff feel ready for the challenge. Becoming involved may also help staff to understand the importance of meetings as a place for learning and not just another hour to be bored (see Chapter 8).

Finally, consider having staff personal development files. These records are particularly useful for trainee staff who can use the information collected as evidence for their NVQ Awards. Make sure that trainee staff keep their training programmes and are able to reflect on what they have learned to prove that they were awake during the course!

Include the following sections in the personal development files:

➤ job descriptions
➤ person specifications
➤ qualifications
➤ specific roles and responsibilities, for example, SENCO or Health and Safety Officer
➤ training applications
➤ attendance at training events
➤ annual development appraisal.

Supervising and appraising staff

Managers have a duty to develop expertise in people who have different roles and responsibilities, are at various stages of development and have different expectations of the job. You need to be able to critically analyse the range of skills and abilities that are necessary for staff to work effectively and you have to help them develop these.

Supervision

In the early years some of this work is done by 'supervision', which gives staff an opportunity to have one-to-one time with their managers to discuss their personal development, review their progress, seek advice and support to help them do their job, and share personal issues. The meeting is confidential and usually takes one hour.

Settings are advised to have a supervision policy to help them ensure that all staff are aware of their rights and responsibilities with regards to supervision, particularly with regards to how information discussed during supervision is shared, recorded and stored (see the photocopiable sheets 'Supervision policy' on pages 153–155 for a sample supervision policy).

A supervision meeting usually takes place every six to eight weeks and should be held in a quiet room. Make sure that you will not be disturbed, unless there is an emergency. You should take notes in a way that will not distract the staff member when he or she is talking. Afterwards you both need to sign the notes and you should keep a copy each. Ensure that the supervision notes are locked safely away so that no one else will see them. The only time these notes should be shared is if they are used as part of the evidence for a disciplinary or grievance hearing and, in this event, the personnel manager may also have a copy.

Supervision meetings are a good time to establish a positive relationship with your staff, to get to know them better and to share something of yourself with them. However, remember that the meetings offer an opportunity for staff members to have their say, so the emphasis has to be on what they want to talk about. Staff are expected to bring items to the agenda, and if there is something that you want to raise with them, such as practice issues or lateness, agree at the beginning of the meeting on how you will balance the range of subjects to be discussed and which of the items can wait for another meeting or could be dealt with quickly.

Carried out well, these meetings are a time for managers to assess staff development and address areas for celebration and improvement. Supervision is a good time to agree on development objectives and action needed to reach them. In agreeing on the targets, you need to take account of individual learning styles, current demands and responsibilities, and available resources.

Supervision must be conducted so as to lead to positive performance. This requires managers to have job-related competence and good communication and people skills. You need your staff to trust you and respect your work. In supervision as in any other area of work, you are a positive role model. It is not good practice to use supervision to talk about yourself and your problems, or to berate and condemn staff.

These meetings will provide an opportunity to praise and celebrate staff achievements, measure their success against their action plans and prepare them for their next challenge. Make supervision a motivating experience so that staff members emerge full of enthusiasm and confidence. Use the photocopiable sheet 'Supervision review form' on page 156 to help staff identify their key targets for development.

Appraisals

Annual reviews of performance, or 'appraisals', should be a positive and productive element of management. They are an excellent way for staff to gain recognition for their hard work and their contribution to the overall success of the setting. They offer every team member the opportunity to discuss the future shape of their career.

Appraisal systems have been adopted by many settings as a method of regularly reviewing how an individual is performing in their job and as a means of assessing their contribution to the organisation. While there are many models for appraisal, Randell et al (1984) state that they could be divided into three broad categories:

➤ performance reviews, which analyse past performance with a view to improving future performance
➤ potential reviews, which assess suitability for promotion and/or future training
➤ reward reviews, which determine salary.

In the past, appraisals got a bad name when they were linked to salaries, and staff were very worried that they may be demoted or have a reduced salary as a result of a negative annual appraisal. However, in the early years, appraisals have never been reflected in staff salaries. They have generally been used to help managers build strong relations with their staff and to find out valuable information about training needs, staff ambitions and concerns.

Appraisals need to be regular, usually once or twice a year, and they should be a positive, objective and constructive process. The successful implementation of an appraisal scheme depends largely on careful planning and acceptance by the staff involved. It is important to recognise that many workers have a negative view of appraisal, so it is essential that the staff in your setting see the benefits and relevance of introducing such a scheme. It is vital to stress the link between appraisal and staff development, as it is an evaluative process that reinforces judgements regarding performance development needs.

The role of appraisal is significant as a motivator and esteem booster. Although managers in early years will be constantly reviewing and evaluating their staff in the natural course of their work, informal appraisal of staff can often be unconscious and subjective. A formal appraisal system will improve the process and ensure that it serves the needs of the setting as well as of the individual.

Consider these things:

➤ setting up your own scheme
➤ selling it positively
➤ telling staff that their salaries will not be affected
➤ thinking carefully about who will be involved in the programme
➤ who will do the appraisals (the line manager, personnel specialist or outsider)
➤ agreeing on whether staff members' performance is to be rated against targets, personal objectives or agreed goals
➤ a pilot team so that you can test the programme, identifying and repairing snags in order to get the programme right for the majority
➤ the format of the appraisal – appraisals are serious meetings
➤ who will have a copy of the appraisal form
➤ will there will be an opportunity to set SMART objectives for future performance?
➤ ensuring that there is a six-month review
➤ agreeing on the time plan for appraisals – are they to be carried out at the end of the calendar year, or at the end of the financial year to fit with the new budget planning?
➤ is there an appeals procedure or can a staff member use the existing grievance procedure if they feel that the process was handled unfairly?

Make the appraisal form a staff training and development annual review. Devise it so that it enables you to collect all the relevant information and provides a focus for the meeting. (For an example of a form, see the photocopiable sheets 'Staff annual development appraisal' on pages 157 and 158.)

Be positive – an appraisal meeting is not the place to raise practice issues, these should have been dealt with earlier. The focus of appraisal is to reflect on success, identify areas for improvement and plan how to meet those and extend potential. Use the photocopiable sheet 'Annual personal development plan' on page 159 to set the focus for the appraisal.

Staff annual development appraisal

Name: *Sunita Keen*
Job title: *Nursery Officer*
Date of appraisal: *21 March 2002*
Length of time in post: *18 months*

All training courses attended this year, including twilight, distance-learning and evening courses:

Date	Course title	Course structure (internal/external/workshop/ twilight/distance learning/evening)	Outcome (award/certificate and so on)
15 May 2001	Paediatric First Aid	External	
23 July 2001	Outdoor play	Internal twilight course	
3 September 2001	Supervising students	External	
15 January 2002	Writing reports more effectively	Internal	

What were your key learning and development achievements in 2001?
More confident dealing with children's accidents (confirmed by positive comments from parents and HSO). Better-planned outdoor sessions (supported by encouraging report from OFSTED). Understanding of how adults learn and my role supporting work-place learning. More effective reports (good feedback from SENCO and college tutor).

Review of the achievements listed above
What was most challenging about your achievements? Why?
I was worried about having learning contract meetings with students, as I was anxious that I did not know enough to share my knowledge with them. Very scared of meeting the tutor as I am shy and was worried that my interim reports about student progress would not be good enough.

What was the most satisfying aspect of your achievements? Why?
I realised that I knew a lot about childcare and education and that my practice was quite sound, although I always have something new to learn. The report-writing course helped me to plan a good report so that it was logical, clear and well presented.

How have you applied your new skills/knowledge at work?
I am going to take two new students this term and I have been invited to the college to talk to potential students about life in a nursery. I can't believe that I am able to do this. It really amazes me that I have the confidence to do this.

What support/resources helped you to achieve this?
Supervision, writing course, student supervisor course, supervisors' meetings.

Encourage your staff to write their personal strengths and weaknesses regarding how they are meeting their achievements (see the sample staff annual development appraisal on page 35). Use the appraisal form to create a climate of reflection and evaluation, encouraging the staff member to identify their own skills. For example, organising an outing successfully will mean that they have gathered information, planned, organised time, made a decision, considered a budget, applied an understanding of health and safety, shared information and communicated with others. Also encourage the staff member to give examples of where they have used the same skills in different circumstances (transferable skills).

Place an emphasis on a balance of qualities and skills. That way there can be no weaknesses – just qualities that are out of balance.

A quality becomes a strength when it is right for you and the situation. A quality becomes a weakness when it is either overdone or underdone for the situation.

Too little	Quality	Too much
Disorganised	Organised	Bossy
Unreliable	Reliable	Becoming indispensable
Closed mind	Open mind	Vague
Slow	Quick to act	Rash

Once you have found a particular quality that is overdone or underdone, you may want to consider steps to bring it into balance.

The main characteristics of any appraisal system will include:

➤ assessment of current performance objectives
➤ assessment of past performance
➤ help to improve current performance
➤ solutions to performance difficulties
➤ assessment of training and development needs
➤ discussion of career opportunities.

Dealing with under-performance

Personal difficulties and work-place problems are both potential causes of demotivation at work. Look out for signs of demotivation and problems among your staff. Invite them to talk about what demotivated them, and listen carefully. Aim to find the root cause of repeated complaints, and eradicate it quickly.

Never ignore your staff's personal problems as they always affect their work. You have to help them find a solution so that they can balance their needs with their ability to do the job. Ultimately, you have to ensure that they do their job properly, so do not wait for their problems to blow over – they might not, and the consequences of failing to deal with a problem will be greater.

Occasionally you may need to apply the disciplinary policy (see Chapter 5). This often helps staff to focus on the issue and gives a helpful framework within which to respond to the problem. Managers are often reluctant to use the disciplinary policy but it can be a very useful tool. Be firm but fair when you are dealing with issues of poor performance. Under-performance is expensive, and yet 85 per cent of all recorded under-performance is thought to result from the systems imposed by the managers. Every work system can have a demotivating effect on staff, so look carefully at the systems that you use. When you introduce new systems, be prepared to use them yourself as well. Treat any feedback from staff seriously and make sure that you respond constructively. However, remind the staff to be constructive in the way that they share concerns too. Comments such as, 'We just don't like it' in response to 'Why don't you like the term "afternoon activities"?' is not helpful as it does not solve the problem. Ask the staff to find an alternative suggestion and remind them that you do not object to changing the term but that they must be more constructive if they want change.

The lessons of failure are valuable, not only to the individuals involved, but also to the setting. Discuss the reasons for failure, so that you can eliminate them and strengthen the likelihood of success in the future. By taking a constructive and sympathetic attitude to failure, you will motivate and encourage your staff. If you choose to punish failure or motivate by fear, you will not create lasting success. However, make it clear that tolerance of error has its limits. Repetition of the same error is inexcusable, since it shows failure or inability to learn from mistakes.

NVQ in Management Level 3 links

Elements	Knowledge evidence	Personal competencies
C7.1 Contribute to identifying personnel requirements	C7.1 and C7.2 Communication Information handling Legal requirements	Acting assertively Behaving ethically
C7.2 Contribute to selecting required personnel	Organisational context Recruitment and selection	Building teams Communicating
C9.1 Contribute to the identification of development needs	C9.1 to C9.4 Communication Continuous improvement Information handling	Influencing others Searching for information
C9.2 Contribute to planning the development of teams and individuals	Involvement and motivation Organisational context Training and development	Thinking and taking decisions
C9.3 Contribute to the development activities		
C9.4 Contribute to the assessment of people against development objectives		

Case studies

Below are two case studies that could be used as staff-meeting discussion points. Talk about what you would do, why you would do it, what policies and procedures you would use to support your decision and why.

Sarah is a nursery nurse in your setting and has been a very reliable worker for the past four years. However, over the past few months she has been late on several occasions and is having regular days off sick. She refuses to discuss the issue and you are worried about her. What do you do? Why? What policies and procedures will you use to deal with the issue?

Things to consider:

➤ training policy and strategy
➤ supervision policy
➤ special leave arrangements
➤ personal action plans
➤ induction programme
➤ staff training and development form
➤ disciplinary procedures from stage one to the outcome
➤ attitude of the other staff
➤ balance between home and work life
➤ the benefits of keeping Sarah with the company given her previous work
➤ keeping records.

Harry is a new manager who is worried about supervising staff. He has one member of staff who always says everything is OK and then does not engage in the rest of the meeting. What should he do? Why? What policies and procedures should he use to deal with the issue?

Things to consider:

➤ supervision policy
➤ barriers to learning
➤ job description
➤ personal action plans
➤ induction programme.

Useful information

➤ Learning and Skills Council, Cheylesmore House, Quinton Road, Coventry CV1 2WT. Tel: 0870-900 6800 (general enquiries helpline). Website: www.lsc.gov.uk

➤ Chartered Institute of Personnel Development, see details on page 16.

Chapter 3 Managing the day

> ➤ **Establishing a routine**
> ➤ **Managing the curriculum**
> ➤ **Linking the routine and the curriculum**
> ➤ **Involving staff in using the routine**
> ➤ **Planning**
> ➤ **Managing recording and assessment**
> ➤ **Policies and procedures**
> ➤ **Working with parents and carers**

How many times have you, as manager, realised that procedures that were in place were not actually being implemented? How often have you assumed that, because it was decided at a staff meeting, things would be done in the agreed format consistently and correctly, only to find that this was not the case? Ensuring that other people do things efficiently and correctly is the key to good management, but it is no mean feat.

There are times when you may feel that you are the only person who can be trusted to do things properly. But if you become involved with every task, you will no longer be able to do your own job, which is to create an environment where everyone works together to get things done in a supportive and motivated way. It is vital that the setting operate smoothly, whether you, the manager, are there or not. An effective manager will understand this and realise that they have to create an environment where this happens. This requires you to create a trusting atmosphere where your staff feel important and valued and are sufficiently trained and supported, so that each staff member gets on with their job and even develops it further. The staff have to show you that you can trust them and you have to be able to relinquish some of your power by delegating and sharing key information, so that your staff have the information and confidence to actually get on with the job.

Establishing a routine

In order for the day to run smoothly, there must be a routine where everyone knows what must happen, when it must happen and why it must happen. The shape of the routine will reflect your specific setting and will take into account the space available, time, number of staff, number of children, available resources, type of children, type of community, access to outside play and whether you operate group care, home care or a classroom.

'Routine' is a word that is often treated lightly and certainly not with the same reverence as the term 'curriculum'. Yet, the routine is critical and is the webbing that pulls everything together. The routine is often seen only as the framework within which the key

domestic activities are plotted, for example, arrival activities, registration, snack time, tidy-up time, outside play, bathroom time, story time, music time and home time.

However, the shape of the routine also sets the ethos of the environment. For example, if the routine is designed to have a lot of free play, the setting will have a particular feel; if on the other hand the routine is designed around adult-directed activities, there will be a different ambience. There is no right or wrong routine in that each setting has to consider its own situation. The agreed routine must then be implemented and evaluated. One key feature of all routines is that they must be underpinned by the principle of equal opportunity so that each child's individual needs are met and staff work sensitively and knowledgeably with diversity.

Managing the curriculum

The early years curriculum is not one whole but is made up of a lot of different parts, in particular:

➤ the philosophy of the setting
➤ the ages and stages of the children
➤ content of learning
➤ resources
➤ social and cultural values of everyone involved in the setting
➤ parental input and expectations
➤ teaching and learning styles.

Whatever the make-up of the setting, the curriculum needs to be developmentally appropriate and sufficiently challenging to extend the children's horizons and to help them recognise their own potential and competence. It needs to have breadth, balance and differentiation.

The curriculum needs to be available to all children, and every effort should be made to include all children by reducing barriers to learning, creating an inclusive environment and celebrating diversity. Staff need to be able to apply anti-discriminatory practice in all their interactions with the children, parents and other adults. They must understand and develop an anti-bias curriculum so that all the children are taught to co-operate and care for one another in an atmosphere of mutual respect and support.

Your setting must reflect the local and wider community through its resources, activities, décor, topics and experiences available to the children. In addition, to ensure that the staff understand the complexity of the anti-bias curriculum and the impact that subconscious attitudes and misunderstanding can have on the long-term welfare of all the children, managers need to make sure that the staff receive regular training and support. This will ensure that they understand and can positively contribute to the service, to reinforce and extend your anti-discriminatory approach.

In her report, Rumbold (1990) suggested that the aims of the curriculum are more likely to be met if staff:

➤ are skilled and very informed, and have high expectations of the children
➤ value the children's parents as the children's first educators
➤ ensure that parents and carers are encouraged to play an active part in their children's care and education.

Curriculum check-list
Ask your staff if they could demonstrate their understanding of the following
aspects of the curriculum:

➤ It ties in fully with the ethos of the organisation.
➤ It provides for all areas of the children's development, for example, if you provide
for babies and after-school children, you will have a separate baby curriculum and
another for the after-school children. As their needs are vastly different, the
curriculum will need to reflect this.
➤ It is play-based. Many parents may think of 'play' as unstructured and aimless, so
be clear about it so that parents know that it is purposeful and supported.
➤ Its content is broad, socially relevant, intellectually challenging and engaging, and
builds on what the children know and can do.
➤ It is designed to ensure that the children consolidate their learning and are ready
to take on new challenges to broaden their skills, knowledge and attitudes.
➤ It helps the children to broaden their skills and builds on their natural curiosity
so that they can see what is possible and develop the confidence to take risks and
try new challenges to become life-long learners.
➤ It supports the children in making links, so that learning is not subject-based but
interconnected to make ideas whole and meaningful, encouraging the children to
learn how to apply their new learning correctly and imaginatively.
➤ It provides opportunities to support the children's home culture and languages,
while also preparing and supporting them to become part of the culture of the
setting and the wider community.

Linking the routine and the curriculum

The daily routine is key to the implementation of the curriculum and will reflect the
philosophy and values of the setting (see the photocopiable sheet 'Setting
philosophy' on page 160 for an example of a setting philosophy). For example, a
setting that is following Montessori principles will have specific activities reflecting
those principles. A setting that has a Froebellian feel may look and be run quite
differently. Every setting will still need to use its routine to provide a frame on which
to plot the activities and experiences of the day.

Most early years settings in England work within the Foundation Stage, which
gives a specific framework through the Early Learning Goals. These must be
developed and extended, so as not to narrow children's opportunities and produce
a watered-down and oversimplified curriculum that would leave children bored,
demotivated and frustrated. Managers need to aim for a broad and balanced
curriculum that helps all children to achieve. It is therefore sensible to design the
routine to give allocated space for regular specific topic activities linked to the Early
Learning Goals. Build in time for planned key group development and assessment
activities in addition to collecting spontaneous observations. Some settings have
planned reading-scheme time and play-based writing and number activities,
particularly where there are children preparing to go to school in the next term, and
these need to feature on the routine as well.

By building curriculum activities into the routine, you will be ensuring that they
are not separate but an integrated part of the daily provision. As part of the routine,
they are also more likely to be completed as required and will stay in the forefront

Manager's tip
Do not
underestimate the
power of the routine.
Recognise that
learning is happening
all the time, and that
it is not about adult-
directed activity time
but the result of
every interaction that
the child has with the
staff and the
environment.

of everyone's minds. By integrating the routine with the curriculum, so that they are intertwined, your staff are more likely to understand that every interaction, however small, routinely domestic or insignificant, plays a vital part in the children's learning.

Informing parents and carers

Parents need to know about your daily routine and understand why it is important to their children. They may not recognise how routine activities can contribute to their learning as many think that learning starts at school and that playing is purely recreational. For this reason they cannot understand why staff seem upset if their child misses activities because they have arrived late at the setting.

Set up a parents' curriculum board to help you communicate with parents, explaining what their children are learning and how this will aid their development. You could send home the photocopiable sheet 'Ideas to try at home' on page 161, filling in the Area of Learning in the left-hand column (for example, 'Creative development') and the activities in the right-hand column ('Painted pictures').

Most parents want the best for their children, and once they understand that you do too and that you have given great consideration to how you will support their children's learning, they usually are very happy to work with you. As a manager, you can help your staff to articulate the reasons behind all requests that are made to parents, whether you are asking for lids of jars for the treasure basket or a photograph of the child's grandparents for some topic work.

Parents need to understand the importance of simple routine rituals such as tidy-up times. It is also helpful for them to know that, for example, Wednesday is 'Show and tell' and Friday is 'Colour day' and why they need to remember to send their child in with a particular object or wearing a sweater in a specific colour. Sometimes, parents misinterpret a routine activity, so staff need to be able to respond clearly and positively to those who complain about their child 'wasting their learning time' picking up toys with which other children have been playing.

Make this sharing of information part of the settling-in process and make it a key theme of a parents' evening. You can also use newsletters to explain the importance of the daily routine and to advise parents on how they can help by doing similar activities at home. Parents often talk with great amusement about how nursery routines are acted out at home when their child insists on being served at supper time or announces that there has been a 'spillage' in the bathroom.

Involving staff and teamwork

The routine usually works better if all the staff are involved in the process of devising it. It also works better if the team has been allowed to test and tweak it until they feel it has begun to work well. The routine has to be embedded in the daily operation of the setting, but staff must understand the concept of flexibility and how and when to use it. For example, the routine always needs to be reviewed when new children join the group – the arrival of two new toddlers may mean that some tweaking to the daily routine is required!

You need to be very aware of whether the routine is actually reinforcing and supporting the team to provide what you have decided is good practice. A routine where you have built in three-hour sleep time for the children so that staff have longer lunch breaks is questionable. However, letting the children watch a short video on a particularly stressful Friday afternoon may well be a preferable option to planned curriculum work.

The routine is also an indicator of the staff dynamics. A newly formed team often has problems with the routine, and a team that could be described as 'dorming', where the staff are settled and cynical, may be operating a routine designed for an easy life with little flexibility and no serious attempts to take account of the children's varying needs. As a manager, being knowledgeable about the routine is vital in order to pick up key indications about the team dynamics and staff morale. Keep the routine dynamic and use it as a lively source of discussion. Having finally agreed on a routine, you may feel entitled to relax, but this should never be the case – there is always room for refinement and new initiatives.

Health and safety

The routine must be underpinned by a clear understanding of health and safety (see Chapter 6 for more information). This is not simply by making sure that spillages are cleared up immediately and that the door is locked securely. Key issues such as supervision of the children, physical care, food hygiene, personal hygiene, storage and waste disposal, chances of cross-infection, management of sick children and evacuation in the event of any emergency, are the shared responsibility of the staff and integral to staff practice – it should not be left just to the health and safety officer (HSO) or to the manager.

Consider building the health and safety annual plan into the routine. Write a list of the key health and safety activities for the month and stick it on the office door. Make sure that there is health and safety time built into the routine and invite the HSO to use it to complete the monthly task, for example, accident-monitoring or checking the fire-drill book. It is also helpful for all staff to be aware of the key monthly tasks, so that they can assist.

Involving staff in using the routine

Show them the big picture

Managers need to have a grasp of the big picture, the organisational vision, but they must also have sound understanding of the operational practicalities faced by staff. You need to be aware of all the issues in order for your staff to have confidence in you. There is nothing more depressing for staff than managers who make unhelpful suggestions or comments or ask inappropriate questions. For example, if there is an issue about staff not sticking to the routine, it is important that you do not make inappropriate suggestions that indicate your lack of knowledge about the children's arrival time or staff lunch breaks. This would simply irritate the staff and they may ignore your guidance.

Know what you want to achieve

A manager needs to have an overall plan in their mind of what they want to achieve each day and over the long term. They must then involve their staff in making it happen. This means giving the staff all the information, being prepared to listen and hear their views, and then agreeing on how and when the routine will be tested and evaluated. When changing the routine, it is always worth letting the new plans run for a month and leaving out a book or page in the diary for staff to scribble in comments where things are not working. Every setting needs an annual development plan, and staff with managerial responsibilities also need their annual plan so that they can be clear about what they want to achieve over the year.

Build a team

For effective teamwork, involve the team in setting key targets. Concentrate on key priorities and help everyone to subscribe to the common goals of the setting and overall aims of the organisation. Emphasise the importance of teamwork and the need to combine everyone's talents to achieve effectively.

Make sure that everyone is aware of their own tasks and responsibilities and of your required standards. Link roles and responsibilities to people's strengths and talents wherever possible. Try to balance the pressures of the team and communicate and share information through regular meetings, consultation and feedback. Give the team some autonomy to make decisions.

Praise the staff members' successes, listen to the team and be loyal to them. No matter how demanding your own routine is, make sure that you get around to everyone and that you monitor all aspects of the team's progress.

Induction

Induct your staff so that they know what is expected of them and what they have to do (see Chapter 2 for more details). Write an induction programme for all your staff, whether they are a manager, deputy, officer, assistant, trainee and so on. Have an induction system for the staff members who are taking on new lead roles such as Health and Safety Officer, SENCO, Pre-school Co-ordinator, key worker, Child Protection Officer or IT Co-ordinator. For an example of an induction programme, see the photocopiable sheets 'Induction programme for a new SENCO' on pages 162–164.

It may be possible to link a new member of staff with the person who previously held the role so that they can help induct the new staff member. However, you need to feel confident that the incumbent of the role is competent to induct the new member correctly. Include a series of questions as part of the induction pack, inviting the new staff member to write the answers, which gives the opportunity for clarification and consolidation of new information. Use one-to-one supervision time to check that they have assimilated the new knowledge.

Develop coaching in the setting to help your staff understand how other people learn. This is very important as they will need to apply new learning during their busy working days. For example, you may wish to encourage them to gain the NVQ Trainer Award.

Have set goals

Managers must set goals. However, these must be balanced to ensure that one goal is not attained at the expense of another. There is no point, for example, in setting a goal for two staff members to manage the snack time while another two tidy up if it does not take into account the likelihood that twice a week there will only be three staff members available.

Communicate clearly with the staff and avoid barriers to communication, such as using jargon, only half-listening and noisy environment.

Delegate

Keep everyone in touch with the main task of the business. In 1930 Chester Barnead, a senior executive of a large American company, carried out lengthy research into successful management techniques and found that staff were much more likely to support the authority of an organisation if they were delegated some authority, so that each individual was responsible for part of the overall enterprise. So managers wanting their team to follow a daily routine could give each staff member some responsibility for one aspect of the routine, with allocated resources or funds and the authority to ensure that other staff are implementing this. For example, one staff member could be given the responsibility for ensuring that circle time happens twice a week. They could be given a small budget to buy suitable resources to give the other staff the incentive to ensure that it happens effectively.

Motivate

Help staff to understand how the daily routine fits into the strategic plan. Give them roles to play to enable them to see how they fit into the routine. For example, consider giving staff lead areas for which they are responsible, including doing the annual audit, from which they can identify what needs to be improved or replaced. It has been found that the more responsibility you give staff, the more they are interested in the outcome.

Delegate relevant decision-making. This motivates people because it gives them a vote of confidence, and decisions that are taken nearer to the point of action are more likely to be correct. If you have a team that is confident, engaged and able to run the day, it reduces the pressure on you, enabling you to get on with other more strategic tasks.

Involve everybody in running the setting well

The manager is ultimately responsible for everything that happens in his or her setting and if there are mistakes, he or she needs to be prepared to take the blame. However, the manager must work hard to make everyone feel equally responsible for the management and development of the service. As the manager, you need to make it the business of everybody that the setting is run well. To do this, you need to be able to understand and motivate your staff – this is a task that can never be underestimated!

Check systems

Managers must keep track of results. There is little point in putting systems in place, requesting that all staff use signing-in sheets or complete activity plans for topic activities twice a week if you never check that this is happening or the results. Think about how all your staff learn and devise a series of checking systems that reflect this: you may use your staff meeting as a training session with colourful props – for example, videos of films such as *Chicken Run* or *Shrek*, which present some significant management issues – or put together an end-of-meeting quiz or multiple-choice questionnaire.

Case studies are also good ways to check if staff are operating within the good practice advocated by the setting. You could also use check-lists or a shared task such as asking the team to make a puzzle or a game that reflects how the routine pulls the whole curriculum together. For example, start a discussion and seek out what people understand by the term 'routine'. Sometimes it is a lack of shared understanding that causes resentments, which can lead to tensions in a team. Ask questions such as, 'What are the principles of a daily routine?', 'How do you adhere to the routine?', 'How do you link the routine into the curriculum?', 'What about health and safety?' and 'Which are the relevant 14 National Standards?'. Remember to praise everyone for meeting routine tasks and do not wait for significant achievements to say 'thank you'.

Planning

Good planning is vital for making children's learning effective. Planning ensures that the needs of children are met and that all the information collected about the children's likes, interests, abilities, additional learning needs and competence is taken into account, so as to move each child forward in a positive and encouraging way. Good planning gives staff a framework within which to apply all the principles of the curriculum.

Planning is often based on topic work and linked to the Early Learning Goals, covering topics such as 'All about me', 'Growing', 'Minibeasts', 'Under the sea', 'Shapes' and 'Numbers'. These topics will cover many areas of the curriculum and are sufficiently broad to include a wide range of activities to meet all the children's needs. This is very important in settings where the children's age ranges span from two years old up to five years old, where some may have special educational needs or English as a second language.

The manager needs to be familiar with the principles of planning and be able to understand long-term (annual overview), medium-term (termly) and short-term (daily implementation and the routine) planning.

Every setting has its own approach to planning, but you must ensure that all the staff understand the approach and can complete the relevant planning forms. There has been a tendency to make planning very complicated and paper-based but it need not be so. Planning is a collection of focused activities and experiences that are designed to help children work towards a goal. For example, the activity may be a photographic record of what happens at key times during the day, and the plan may have been written to help the children consider the concept of sequence. The same activity could also be planned with different outcomes, including developing the children's turn-taking skills, extending vocabulary, practising cutting and sticking, making a group display, encouraging conversation and so on. The aim is that staff know what they want the children to work towards and can plan to achieve this. For practical information on how to plan an early years curriculum, see the *Goals for the Foundation Stage* series (Scholastic).

Managers have to:

➤ have regular planning meetings
➤ create documentation that is self-explanatory
➤ ensure that all information about all the children is taken into account
➤ link any specific Early Action individual education plans into the planning
➤ focus on specific key words to begin with, to ensure that all the children have a full grasp of at least five verbs, nouns and adjectives
➤ include a section on the documentation for extending activities to meet the needs of more able children
➤ provide an introduction to the planning process for new staff

➤ use terms such as 'teaching techniques' and 'learning strategies' to help staff recognise what this means

➤ ensure that staff plan for both indoors and outdoors

➤ provide staff with useful resource books to extend their ideas

➤ ensure that planning is linked to the routine, such as topic-based activities

➤ involve parents and carers

➤ help staff to understand the importance of evaluating the planning process so that they can make necessary adjustments

➤ be prepared to change a topic if the staff and children find it inappropriate or boring, or if something more engaging and relevant happens.

Managing recording and assessment

Assessment is a key function of a child's education. Most of early years assessment is based on observation, applying different observational techniques where appropriate. The manager has the task of ensuring that staff:

➤ understand the importance of observation

➤ understand the principles of observation

➤ can apply different techniques, including one-to-one conversations with the children to seek their views about their own progress

➤ create a shared system for recording observations, such as observation books in each area, having a 'child of the week', planned assessment activities where key workers assess key skills, or using a video

➤ build in 'write up' time so that key workers have time to collate all the observation evidence

➤ have a child record book, profile or record of achievement that gives clear guidance as to how observations are recorded and what kinds of supporting evidence will be included. Staff generally prefer a system, especially when they are responsible for a large number of key children. A blank page can be very intimidating and by leaving too much leeway for what information will be gathered you will often find a great deal of inconsistency. Parents may notice this and may link the quality of the children's records to the quality of the provision.

Policies and procedures

All routines need to be underpinned by a set of clear and consistent policies and procedures. Have a well-ordered operational manual that is divided into logical sections such as 'Health and safety', 'Arrival and collection', 'Fees', 'Forms', 'Staff information' and so on. Alternatively, you could use the same headings as the National Standards, for example, 'Equipment', 'Safety', 'Health' and so on, as this will help you to see how you meet the National Standards within your daily routine. This manual will be in addition to the relevant policy folders, such as the health and safety folder and the staff personnel handbook.

Divide the notice-board into key areas, for example, 'Health and safety', 'Policy of the month', 'Pre-school minutes', 'Management-meeting minutes', 'SENCO-meeting minutes' and 'Staff-meeting agenda'. When notices are pinned up, they will be easy to see, especially if they are colour-coded, and staff can sign and date the documents to indicate that they have read them. This way, you will not need to

Manager's tip

If you carry out a random staff survey, you may find that many people's greatest anxiety is writing up records, which explains why they are often overdue or incomplete. Put together sample material and give regular workshops to all staff. You may have to put on additional report-writing courses and computer training to give staff the basic writing skills. Staff may say that limited time is the reason for failure to complete records, but this may be a foil for a deeper anxiety.

chase staff to check if they have read the minutes, and you can pick up who is always last to sign or fails to sign the forms.

Have a system for updating folders to make sure that everyone has the same information. Build in questions on where to find certain information into the staff induction pack. Write the curriculum policies in a way that your staff can see how they are linked to the daily routine and the everyday interaction between staff, children and parents. When devising a new policy, add a quiz or check-list, so that the staff have to check their own understanding of what they have read. Put a policy on the staff-meeting agenda once a month for discussion, or as the source of a case study, so that the staff have to apply their knowledge of the policy to a situation. This is a very good management checking system. Complete policy and procedures adherence forms to confirm that staff have read and understood the information, or ask them to sign their own copies of key policies. Review this at regular intervals.

What are policies and procedures?

A policy is the course of action adopted by the organisation that tells you what you would do in particular circumstances. The procedures are the stages by which you meet the policy requirements. Practice is the application of policy. Good policies are underpinned by theory and research and aim to promote high standards.
Having a policy that is consistently adhered to by all staff gives clear messages about practice and procedure, thus avoiding misunderstandings and discrepancies. All staff will know what is expected of them and how to respond as necessary. When writing or reviewing policies it is a good idea to form a working party of staff. By involving the staff you will improve accountability and this is also a useful training exercise as it helps to explore the subject of the policy.

Before writing a policy

Before beginning to look at a policy, decide why you want it. Is it to inform staff, to guide them or as a source of information? If policies are to be used in large organisations, or those settings that are part of a group, then it makes sense to agree on a policy format, which may contain:

➤ an introduction
➤ an aim
➤ ways of achieving the aim
➤ the role of the adult
➤ a review and audit.

Before writing a policy, and when reviewing existing ones, check the relevant legislation, the National Standards requirements (issued from the Care Standards Act 2000), recent research on good practice issues, and health and safety requirements.

How to write a policy

In order to write a policy you will need to:

➤ research the area
➤ seek the advice of specialists or the Early Years Development and Childcare Partnership advisory teachers

➤ talk to colleagues in other settings – they may share their policies with you
➤ involve the staff, ask for their advice and delegate some research tasks to interested staff members
➤ talk to parents and carers and seek their views, particularly if you have parent representatives (give them the draft for comment)
➤ avoid using jargon that could make the policy an unnecessarily daunting document that staff will not read
➤ consider how you will share the information with parents and others and how you will ensure that all staff know about it
➤ write a first draft and circulate it for comments, giving a return-date deadline and then using the information that is returned positively.

For an example of guidance on how to write a special needs policy, see the photocopiable sheets 'Special educational needs policy' on pages 165–167.

Key policies and procedures needed

It is wise to have policies on the following areas to help you to manage the day:

➤ admissions
➤ babies
➤ child protection
➤ children's records
➤ complaints
➤ confidentiality
➤ curriculum, which may be linked to the Early Learning Goals
➤ equal opportunities
➤ food and drink, and food hygiene
➤ health and safety
➤ managing children's behaviour
➤ partnership with parents, including a parents' information pack
➤ personnel handbook
➤ planning
➤ recruiting and selecting staff
➤ settling in
➤ special needs (in line with the new *Code of Practice*)
➤ students
➤ supervision and appraisal
➤ waiting-list.

These should be stored, labelled and accessible to all staff. This list is not exhaustive but it meets all the requirements of the 14 National Standards.

You should also have a policy on the administration of medicines and managing ill children that clearly states your position on infectious illnesses, antibiotics, notifiable illnesses and non-prescribed medicines, including teething gels and homeopathic remedies. With notifiable illnesses, you may need to inform the Environmental Health Service, usually based at the Local Education Authority headquarters. Some settings will be required to display information about the illness for all parents and carers, and in some settings fees are waived for children absent with notifiable illnesses.

In addition, the administration of medicine policy must include the setting's procedure for accepting children with allergies and the administration of inhalers and other emergency invasive medicines. The Care Standards Act 2000 requires that staff administering emergency treatment, such as inhalers, epinephrine auto-injectors (for severe allergic reactions) or rectal diazepam (in the case of children prone to severe fits), be trained by a medical practitioner. It is no longer sufficient for a parent to show the staff what to do in the event of an emergency. Some hospitals have a community nursing team and they will offer this training at a low or no cost.

Working with parents and carers

The manager's job, with the staff team, is to create an atmosphere and service that support each parent's desire for their child to be happy in the setting. It is vital to give a positive first impression of your group, whether it is through your welcome pack, a telephone enquiry, your website or a first visit to the setting.

Parents and carers are generally the setting's greatest advocates, so your first contact with them is very important. Make sure that your staff are well trained and understand the complexity of working with parents. This includes accepting that the basis of any staff–parent relationship is that the child belongs to his or her parents and that the setting will work with them to support their child's learning and development. This view can sometimes get lost when staff work in settings where parents have complicated emotional lives. It is true that sometimes parents need to be reminded that children are not quite as resilient as they think and their attention has to be re-directed back to the child. This sensitive work has more chances of success if parents have developed a mutually respectful and trusting relationship with the staff.

Successful communication

Have a clear philosophy, or statement of principles, so that parents know what the expectations of the setting are. For example, if you say that you are an 'open access' setting, explain what this means. If parents think that it means that they can call in at any time and talk to staff, whereas you mean 'Come and visit any time but access to staff is not generally available at all times', then you need to make it explicit.

For children who are new to your group, have a thorough settling-in procedure and make sure that all staff operate it consistently, giving correct information to parents and carers. There is nothing more unnerving for parents than receiving mixed messages, so make sure that all communications are clear and consistent. Let them have suggestions for helpful ways in which they can prepare their children for the new setting and make a list of information that the setting will need in advance (see page 51 for an example).

Check-list for the children's information forms

The nursery must keep certain records as a requirement of the law. These must include details of the children and information about their developmental and educational progress. All information is shared with the parents or carers.

➤ Be quite clear about your policies and procedures. Every setting needs to have rules and regulations, so be prepared to share your reasons for them and then apply them fairly and rationally. Parents soon pick up any hint of favouritism.

What	When	Why	Who
Admission form	Before starting	To ensure that key information is available.	Parents and key worker
Terms and conditions	Before starting	To agree on expectations and clarify any queries. Reserve the right to ask a parent to leave if they contravene the terms or operate in a discriminatory or aggressive manner.	Parents, nursery manager and key worker
Settling-in form	First day	To get specific information about the child.	Key worker and parent
Child record card	First day	Immediate information.	Key worker and parent
Home–nursery parent partnership agreement	During settling period	To clarify shared expectations and responsibilities.	Parent, nursery manager and key worker
Observation forms	Ongoing and recorded quarterly	To monitor the child's development, to note concerns, attendance and comments from staff, parents and child, and to inform planning.	Key worker
Review form	Approximately six weeks after settling in	To establish if the child and parents have settled in and to agree on the next stage.	Nursery manager and key worker
My life in nursery book	Begin after three months	To record development against the key learning areas, build the child's knowledge, celebrate their achievements, and assess and monitor their progress.	Key worker

➤ If the setting is an inclusive setting, make the special needs policy very public. Explain what it means and be honest about the impact that there may be on the setting when a child with specific special needs joins. There may be no effects for the children in the group, but as soon as any child starts behaving in a disruptive way parents will complain, irrespective of the child's age, stage or situation! Your staff may find themselves in a very uncomfortable position, defending the right of all children to attend a mainstream setting, but acknowledging that some behaviour is consistently anti-social and can appear very threatening. Interestingly, children often cope much better than their parents, but they will be influenced by their parents' attitudes, and the situation of a child being blamed for everything bad even when he or she is not there is one all early years staff have encountered.

➤ Prepare your staff, ensuring that they are well trained and can answer complaints such as, 'Why is she screaming/snatching/hitting her head/biting?'. It is unfair but it is only negative behaviour that usually elicits responses.

➤ Encourage parents and carers to participate in your activities such as fund-raising, sharing ideas, accompanying the children on outings, contributing to the topic and operating a shared approach to their child's care and education. Remember to include parents with English as an additional language, those from a minority cultural group and those who have full-time jobs and have difficulty finding time to be involved.

➤ Encourage fathers to become involved too. Look at successful models such as the one at the Pen Green Centre (see 'Useful information' on page 54) and adopt policies to include male family members.

Ways to keep in touch

Identify your methods of communication. The most useful kind may be face to face on a daily basis and you should encourage this, but also have back-up systems:

➤ a white-board with daily information written on. This is useful for information such as 'Sally on annual leave today and Roua from the agency is covering. The dental nurse is visiting today and remember Wednesday is red day, so don't forget to dress your child in something red. Thank you'.

➤ newsletters, with a regular addendum providing a list of where all written information can be found. For example, 'In the main hall you will find the weekly topic planning board. Inside to the left you will find the lunch menus. On your child's coat-peg there is a bag in which all parents' letters will be placed for collection at pick-up time. In the yellow room there are sleep charts. On the bathroom door there is the nappy-changing rota.'

➤ parents' evenings

➤ a parents' handbook including information about the philosophy, curriculum, routine, activities, outings, terms and conditions, illness and fees for the setting. Include a question-and-answer section addressing issues such as, 'What happens if my child has an accident?', 'Can my child bring toys and sweets to nursery?' and 'Can I give the staff a thank-you present?'.

Information and feedback

If you use a key-worker scheme, make it clear what this means and what a key worker does. Avoid creating dependency by a child on one member of staff, particularly as the key worker may be absent some of the time. Emphasise that all staff aim to know all the children well but that the key-worker system is critical to the settling-in process for parents and children.

Make a complaints procedure available, but emphasise the importance of resolving any concerns through discussion wherever possible. You may need to constantly clarify parental expectations.

Remember that staff meetings and in-service training may impact on parents and carers directly because of early or full closures or changes of staff, so explain the importance of keeping staff informed and up to date with training issues.

Try to think of effective ways of getting feedback from parents and carers. Some early years settings that are part of a quality assurance programme will already do this, but the Government has set a target according to which 40 per cent of all settings receiving Government funding will need to be part of an approved quality assurance scheme by 2004, so it is worth considering the issue of meaningful feedback.

Manager's tip

Be aware of your own perspective and values and how these influence your practice. Be open to learning new information and be respectful of others whose perspective or values differ from your own.

Do not be frightened of feedback. If you ask for it, be prepared for the fact that some may be negative. Really listen and review your procedures or attitudes, especially if you receive a lot of similar comments.

Include a statement in your handbook about child protection. Make it clear that the setting will deal with incidents or suspicions that a child may be at risk of harm immediately and effectively. Ensure that there is a statement about how children's negative behaviour is dealt with in the setting. It could be part of the personal, social and emotional policy or you may choose to have a separate behaviour policy. The former may be more positive because the emphasis can be placed on reducing and avoiding negative behaviour rather than 'dealing with it'.

NVQ in Management Level 3 links

Elements	Knowledge evidence	Personal competencies
A1.1 Maintain work activities to meet requirements	*A1.1* Communication Customer relations Involvement and motivation Monitoring and evaluation Organisational context Planning	Acting assertively Building teams Communicating Focusing on results Influencing others
B1.1 Make recommendations for the use of resources	*B1.1* Analytical techniques Communication Involvement and motivation Organisational context Resource management	Managing self Searching for information Thinking and taking decisions
C4.1 Gain the trust and support of colleagues and team members	*C4.1* Communication Information handling Organisational context Providing support Working relationships	
D1.1 Gather required information *D1.2* Inform and advise others *D1.3* Hold meetings	*D1.1* to *D1.3* Analytical techniques Communication Information handling Leadership styles Meetings Organisational context	
C9.3 Contribute to development activities	*C9.3* Continuous improvement Training and development	

Case studies

Below is a selection of case studies that could be used as staff-meeting discussion points. Talk about what you would do, why you would do it, what policies and procedures you would use to support your decision and why.

➤ A parent complains about tidy-up time saying, 'I didn't send my child to nursery to help put things away. This is the responsibility of the staff.' How do you respond? How do you prepare your staff to respond?

➤ A member of staff says that there is a lot of 'dead time' in the routine. What do you think she means? How will you address it?

➤ You have had a major flood in the setting that has resulted in a lot of upheaval and redecoration. During that time you were flexible with the routine and key group work, and focused outdoor activities were carried out quite sporadically. The setting is back to normal now but the staff are still acting as if it was not. What do you do?

➤ Ms Howard has a child in your setting who attends regularly and is making good progress. However, despite this, she appears not to be satisfied with the service. She complains that her child is learning nothing and spends her time running around. She says, 'I don't want any of this free-expression rubbish'. How could you respond to this?

➤ You have noticed that one of the most senior staff in your team has difficulty getting certain tasks completed on time. Activity sheets, training forms and child-development reports are always late or simply not completed. Quite often when they are finished they are scrappy, badly written and poorly presented. This staff member is solid, reliable and very competent in many other aspects of her job.

Consider what to do with regards to:

➤ procedures for addressing the issue
➤ how to communicate the issue at all levels, taking account of each person's perspective and how they are feeling
➤ indicators of barriers to accepting your views
➤ the impact that your management style may have on the result
➤ management checking systems
➤ helpful management theories
➤ other issues.

Useful information

➤ Pen Green Centre for Under Fives and Their Families, Pen Green Lane, Corby, Northamptonshire NN17 1BJ. Tel: 01536-400 068. Website: www.btinternet.com/~pengreen

Manager's handbook   *early years* **training & management**

Chapter 4 Managing change

> ➤ **Why change?**
> ➤ **Understanding the impact of change**
> ➤ **Creating a setting that can cope with change**
> ➤ **Sample change action plan**
> ➤ **Implementing the change**
> ➤ **The impact of change on the manager**
> ➤ **Monitoring change**

Managing change is part of life. Change can come from anywhere and no one can escape the impact of societal, political and demographic trends. In an early years setting, change can come from inside and outside, from staff, parents, other users of the service and from within a management hierarchy. Wherever it comes from, managers have to be ready to respond and deal with change, so that the outcome is positive. Over the last few years, all early years settings have had to respond to a vast array of Government-led changes to funding, curriculum, service development and partnership with professionals and parents.

It's not the strongest species that survives nor the most intelligent but the most responsive to change.

– Charles Darwin –

There are two main types of organisational change: strategic and operational. The strategic change relates to the future direction of the setting, affecting one or more goals. It involves some major switch in what the setting does, and how it does it, and usually takes place over several years. Operational, or day-to-day, change happens constantly. Managers are either making or responding to events that require change, making adjustments to work practice and the management of the setting.

Change can be frightening, but it does not need to be and it can be very healthy. In order to manage change effectively, you will have to be able to adapt positively to it, understanding the processes involved and their effects on your staff and the running of the setting. You will need to be prepared, sensitive and informed.

Why change?

All organisations need to be able to respond to change in order to remain competitive and viable. Staff have to be able to continually reflect and review their service, to ensure that it is meeting the needs of those using it as well as potential users. Most change that occurs in a setting is instigated from within and will involve fairly minor changes that can be planned for and tested carefully – for example, reviewing the routine to take account of a new child, reorganising the outside area because of the weather, or writing incidents and accidents on just one record sheet instead of two different forms. The best ideas for change are often simple, effective and come from those in the front line, and the change can make life easier for everyone.

There are other times when major strategic changes are imposed because of economic issues. This could be in reaction to new challenges – for example, in early years there is a Government-led demand for more childcare places, but there is also an ongoing recruitment crisis. In order to try to increase places, many settings have massively increased the number of trainees that they employ. This has had a major strategic impact in terms of training, support, staff responsibilities and delegation, and so the balance of workload for the whole team in a setting.

Some early years settings have grown enormously over the past five years. There are now many large nursery chains, after-school clubs have expanded, with the support of Government funding, and membership organisations have also grown. Growth such as this brings change for people within the organisations as well as for those receiving a service. In view of growth, organisations need to consider their ability to transform and then must plan the expansion carefully, so that they are not placed under too much pressure.

Many people see change as a negative process, because it involves engaging with the unknown, but this is not always the case. Change can be a stimulus for new ideas and can rekindle enthusiasm and commitment. In 1927 psychologist Elton Mayo discovered that output increased every time a change was made to working conditions. Also, absenteeism declined by 80 per cent during the period of change. The explanation that he gave was that people responded to attention. Taking part in experiments and co-operating in changes heightens interest, team spirit and self-esteem, regardless of what the change is. He suggested that managers needed to look for ways to engage all their staff in reviewing processes and practices, and in devising ways of changing and correcting practices.

Change management is a critical function of the manager. It requires them to know where they are going and how they intend to get there. This means that they must have a clear and realistic vision for the setting. Understanding this is critical when planning for change, as the change is more likely to be successful if the staff are in sympathy with the plan and can see how their personal values fit with the setting's vision and objectives.

Understanding the impact of change

Change means:

> learning something new
> unlearning what you already know and can do
> challenging your personal attitudes.

Change is not made without inconvenience, even from worse to better.
– Samuel Johnson –

The process of change is challenging, but everyone is capable of change and after a while it becomes hard to remember life before! Remember how many of us were terrified of new technology, yet now we send text messages and chat on mobile phones and use e-mail as if it were the most natural thing in the world.

As the manager, you will have a significant part to play in the management of change. Firstly, you have to understand it and then you have to know how to motivate your staff to accept the change and actually want it. Some companies have avoided redundancies during economic downturn by selling the options for change positively, offering alternatives such as career breaks, sabbaticals and reduced working hours.

While you are implementing change, you must also maintain a sense of purpose, so that your staff feel safe and know where you are leading them. You will need to accept that resistance to change is often the first and most powerful reaction from the staff team. There are certain changes that are very likely to provoke resistance, for example, changes that:

> affect knowledge and skill requirements
> cause financial or status loss

➤ are suggested by staff but that may elicit a jealous response from other staff, who may feel that the new ideas could lead to their loss of esteem
➤ involve risk and increase the possibility of failure
➤ involve social relationships
➤ are unplanned.

Sometimes you have no choice but to implement change. For example, the introduction of the Care Standards Act 2000 and Government funding for three-year-olds has meant some changes in all early years settings. There is little that you can do about these changes except to help your staff understand the change and then respond and cope with it. However, where you are choosing to make changes to practice or procedures, it is worth remembering that change is not helpful if it adds to staff problems.

Responding to change

As a manager, you will need to be able to recognise every member of staff's response to change and never assume that you know how they will respond. For example, if the staff have not made a fuss, do not make the mistake of thinking that they have accepted the change, and bear in mind that quiet defiance is much harder to deal with.

Theorists have observed key patterns of behaviour that are common responses to change. These include:

Shock	Will I have a job?
Anxiety	How will I cope with this? It's all too much.
Denial	I will just ignore it and if I say 'no' often enough they will go away.
Resistance	It will never work.
Fear of overload	I can't manage my work now, how will I do this as well?
Low morale	This is all too much, they do not care about the staff.
Awareness	OK, I recognise it is needed but how will I manage it?
Incompetence and fear of failure	I can't do this.
Sense of loss of control	I will look stupid if I can't do this and I am supposed to be a senior staff member.
Acceptance	I will try, maybe it is possible.
Testing/searching for meaning	I will start to read it and understand what I have to do.
Understanding and adjustments	Let's get on with it, it is not so bad.
Integration	It's OK now, I can work within this.

Manager's tip
Expect emotions to run high. Consider setting up systems of support to reduce negative stress and to reassure your staff. A few changes can make all the difference between a boring work environment and a stimulating one, but too many changes will leave the staff overwhelmed. Poor management of the change could lead to a demotivated team, with the consequences of low morale, tired staff, absenteeism, an increased number of mistakes, confusion and a greater chance of conflict in the setting. Do not be flippant, take everyone's reactions seriously.

Creating a setting that can cope with change

Given that early years settings are constantly subject to change, a solution to help cope with change is to create a dynamic learning environment and organisational culture that embraces change and does not immediately reject the possibility of any change. Such settings tend to be goal-directed and purposeful, and change becomes a habit for everyone. They have a clear balance between autonomy and control, and the constraints are defined and accepted. Staff know what they can do and what is expected of them, and managers inspire the team and foster creativity and innovation.

The development of the setting is a continual activity where change is part of the improvement process. Aim to create an environment in which:

➤ there is a culture of ongoing learning, ensuring that this is written as part of the principles of the setting
➤ it is safe for individuals to try out different ways of doing things, to contribute more fully and to have a greater share in what is going on in the setting
➤ communication is open and frank, ideas are encouraged and tested out, and staff know what happens to their ideas.
➤ decisions are made near to the information point rather than referred up through the hierarchy
➤ everyone's work is valued and people's interdependence is made clear
➤ staff are encouraged to consider their own contributions to the setting, so that their strengths are valued, their personal challenges are identified and opportunities are provided to help them meet such challenges
➤ staff are encouraged to be curious, well informed, up to date and interested to know what is going on in the world outside their setting
➤ there are systems in place to regularly publicise and celebrate the achievements of colleagues.

How to prepare staff for change

Introducing change is a challenge for most settings and managers. Successful change can only happen through people, and people respond best to change when they are involved, because they can then feel that they retain some control over the change. One of the manager's key tasks is to implement change. To do this, you will need to prepare carefully in order to increase the chance of success. McCalman and Paton (1992) suggest that the key to successful change management is to:

➤ define the change
➤ formulate success criteria
➤ identify performance measures
➤ generate options
➤ select appropriate evaluation methods
➤ evaluate options
➤ develop an implementation plan.

Managers must remember to define why the change is needed, be clear about their message, sort out their own worries about the change somewhere else, and not let their anxieties or concerns affect their staff. Their attitude to the change will have a huge impact on the way in which their staff respond.

Sample change action plan

Action needed	Who will do this?	What resources will be needed? (training/finance/time)	Communication methods (as many ways as possible and as often as possible)	Possible problem	Possible solution
To review all current planning sheets	Pre-school co-ordinator and room leaders	All documentation in one file	Change display board with big version of action plan. Everything to do with change will be corresponded on green paper	Establish learning need because some staff cannot use these ones	Workshop and coaching session
To look at the routine and see when we can plan the activities to collect other information for use in child observation records	Deputy manager	One hour free on Tuesday	Minutes of meetings on the change board. Feedback at room meetings. Summary hand-outs of main points for the staff meeting	Time is short and staff busy. Major resistance and anxiety	Cover for allocated time
To prepare a teaching session about why to use the forms	Manager	Completed teaching plan and relevant handouts with main points	Management-meeting discussion	No additional funds in training budget	Apply to EYDCP for advisory teacher support
To talk to staff about the information that they need to have on the forms	Staff working group	Joint room meetings Wed and Fri 10-11. Ask to put it on the agenda	Check-list placed on the change display board in green so it stands out and is easily recognised as part of the change	Not enough time to deal with everything in the meeting	Bring a check-list to consolidate learning
Ask staff to bring different examples of forms to the staff meeting	Manager	Sample forms	Staff-meeting minutes	Misunderstanding and complexity	May be a very good example to use as template
To agree and type up a sample form and pilot it	Manager and staff working group	Administration time, access to office computer and pilot plan with clear SMART targets	Green form devised and circulated to everyone with their names on it. Sample on the change display board	Failure to analyse the progress and risk that the staff may not be fully competent to introduce new model	Set review date and give each member of the pilot a written task

As a manager implementing change, you have to be prepared to help your staff to see what is in it for them, which means that you have to be well versed in all the possibilities that the change will bring (good and bad). Think about how you are going to balance challenge and success so that the change is exciting.

Make an overall plan using the photocopiable sheet 'Change action plan' on page 168. Keep it clear and simple and leave space for people to add details so as to make the plan a shared one, with shared accountability. (See page 59 for a sample change action plan.) Keep a check-list for your own reference using the photocopiable sheet 'Manager's change check-list' on page 169. For example, you could check if the staff know why the change is being implemented, if everyone will get the right information and is sure of their role in the change process, if you are all clear about the timetable and whether it is displayed prominently enough, and, ultimately, whether the change has been achieved. Include obstacles to change and potential problems in the plan. If possible, allocate resources to help you deal with them as they arise. Consider:

➤ if you will need to budget for more cover staff
➤ if the staff will need to work extra hours
➤ if you can build in extra coaching to help the staff learn the new skills
➤ if you have some money available to take your staff for lunch at critical stages of the change process.

Communication strategy

Make sure that you can answer these questions:

1 Why is the change needed?
2 When will you start telling your staff?
3 What will you say and to whom?
4 Where and how will you share the information?
5 If you are managing a change from higher up, how will you keep in regular contact with the staff and share new information?
6 How will you respond to queries and anxieties?
7 How frequently will you update the information?

Be very clear yourself so that you can respond to queries and allay gossip and inaccuracies. Changes in the setting may require staff to learn new ways of doing things. Identify the emerging learning needs and how you will support them. This may be by providing additional coaching and internal or external training. Check your options through your Early Years Development and Childcare Partnership.

Have a meeting with every member of the team and write a personal plan for them, identifying what they will need to cope with the change. Help them to see what they can learn from this new transition.

You may find using a competency model helpful when identifying what skills and knowledge your staff will need to acquire in order to deal with the change. For example, if you are introducing the concept of observation into an after-school setting, you have to know what the staff will need to ensure that they can complete the observational tasks required. Using a competency model may help because it identifies what you need to know, and what you need to be able to do, in order to prove that you have a competent grasp of the subject. In early years this is sometimes sadly lacking and we talk in terms of broad concepts, which is not very helpful for staff who want to know exactly what they need to know and do, in all the relevant contexts, in order to meet the requirements of the job.

Build the new changes into the induction programmes for all new staff and do not be afraid to use the disciplinary procedure if you encounter destructive resistance.

Ten tips

1 Prepare your staff.
2 Let your staff know how things will be after the change.
3 Be honest and flexible.
4 Involve your staff in the process.
5 Communicate little, often and in as many ways as possible.
6 Listen to and respect your staff's feelings.
7 Be enthusiastic and positive.
8 Find out who are the supporters and the resisters, and use their energy positively.
9 Look after the people leading the change.
10 Celebrate the new methods and do not criticise past ones.

Implementing the change

➤ Lead from the top.
➤ Make only the necessary changes. Some change is fundamental but other change is less so.
➤ If possible, have a pilot scheme and try out the change out in a small, controlled group first.
➤ Provide clear, accurate and useful information orally and in writing, using every medium available to you. Consider using slogans, e-mails, updates, newsletters, message boards, staff meetings and link staff. For example, if the change involves working with children who have special needs, bring all your special educational needs co-ordinators on board with the change and involve them in selling it to the other staff members.
➤ Keep the communication channels flowing. You can never give your message too many times. If you think that you have said it too much, say it again! Give out small chunks of information at a time to avoid overload. A little and often seems to be a good balance because it keeps the change on the agenda, but not so that it is overwhelming everything else that is going on.
➤ Make the information personal, such as by telling stories about the impact that the change has had elsewhere. Remember that 80 per cent of an organisation's resources are channelled into formal communications, yet 80 per cent of the impact is at an *informal* level, so get the right balance between formal and informal communication.
➤ Reassure your staff about the impact of the change. Be open and honest and tell them how it will affect their job.
➤ Ask for your staff's support and make it clear what it is that you need them to do. Do not assume that they understand – check to confirm.
➤ Find allies who will support the change and help you to implement it. Invite someone who has been through a similar change elsewhere to talk to the staff. Anecdotes are very popular. Show staff videos of what you want the change to look like. Make it real so that it is not so frightening, especially if it involves technology!

Manager's tip
When implementing change, be ready to:
➤ tune into other people's ideas, views and feelings
➤ invite suggestions from everybody
➤ express your thoughts in a fluent manner using relevant examples to make meanings clear
➤ have frequent formal and informal meetings
➤ adapt how you speak to ensure clear understanding
➤ ask insightful questions
➤ listen attentively
➤ manage people's expectations with care and sensitivity.

➤ If you are giving other people the responsibility to share information, make sure that they know exactly what to say and are able to cope with any questions. If in doubt, do all the briefings yourself.

➤ Give the staff members who are complaining the loudest a key role in the change management.

➤ Keep other areas of the work place stable. People value and need security.

➤ Involve the staff. Do not just say that people can share their views – really listen to them. Have a focus or working group. If you can, set up a change management group to help you manage the change.

➤ Give credit to people's fears and concerns.

➤ Remember that you will have to help individual staff cope with change, and that may require a range of different methods.

➤ Make good use of your problem-solving skills.

➤ Make sure that you have the resources necessary to make the change.

➤ Have clear, realistic time-scales for the implementation of the change.

➤ Put a programme of support coaching and training in place. Provide a range of facilities – everyone has a different learning style.

➤ Be visible and 'walk the job' so that people can talk to you.

➤ Have a celebration to mark the change, particularly if it is a specific change, such as moving to another building, opening a new setting, changing staff team or taking babies for the first time. Some changes, such as reorganising the rooms, changing recording systems or changing staff routines, are more difficult to celebrate, but there is no harm in having extra treats in the staff room and at the next staff meeting, sending the staff individual thank-you cards or setting up a celebratory display.

The impact of change on the manager

The process of change is very demanding and you will need your own support. Implementing change is an emotionally demanding and tiring process. It requires determination, energy, patience, motivation, plenty of sensitivity and effective checking systems. There are many battles to be won, not least the situations where staff agree to make the changes but as soon as you are out of sight revert to previous methods. You also need to be careful not to seem as if you are favouring those who support the change – this could create team divisions and dissent among all staff.

Some managers have no direct support but you will need a champion to help you through. A mentor could provide that support. This person could be a friend or colleague in another setting, a colleague from an advisory team or someone from the Local Authority mentoring programme. A mentor could help in the following ways:

➤ making sense of the impact that the process is having on you and the setting

➤ defining continuing objectives, monitoring progress and solving problems

➤ acting as a consultant adviser or researcher on matters associated with new learning

➤ supporting you so that you increase your skill, confidence and capability

➤ reflecting on the change and supporting you to 'hold your nerve' so that the new practice can embed. This is particularly important as many people may have lost their confidence half-way through the change process and, while some adaptations may be necessary, it is important to see the planned change through.

Manager's tip

How to influence behaviour without burning yourself out:

➤ Set individual objectives for people to keep them focused.

➤ Praise people publicly and privately.

➤ Set high standards and never ignore mistakes.

➤ Make work fun – look for ways to celebrate and stimulate.

➤ Give people supportive opportunities to take on new roles.

➤ Reward hard work and commitment.

➤ Make work conditions comfortable (remember Maslow's hierarchy).

➤ Reinforce new work practices.

Monitoring change

As with all management processes, change needs to be monitored and reviewed to check that it is happening in the way that you intended. Build a review system into the initial plan:

➤ Start by recognising everyone's contributions.
➤ Get feedback in as many ways as possible, such as staff meetings, e-mail, questionnaires, snag sheets, white-board, update information sheets.
➤ Ask all staff and anyone else involved, including children and their parents or carers, the following questions:
  • How do you think the change process was managed?
  • What worked well and why?
  • What was not so helpful and why?
  • What have you learned from the whole process that would influence your approach to the next change challenge?
➤ Make time to observe new practice and talk directly to the staff implementing the change.
➤ Be available to talk through the effects of the change.
➤ Do not give up half-way – every change can feel shaky in the middle.
➤ Encourage your staff to give you suggestions for improvements if there are emerging snags.
➤ Praise and thank the staff for their efforts.
➤ Mark the ending of the change and do not criticise the past, even if the good old days are now so old that no one remembers them!
➤ Reward your staff.

NVQ in Management Level 3 links

Elements	Knowledge evidence	Personal competencies
C4.1 Gain the trust and support of colleagues and team members	C4.1 and C4.3 Communication Information handling Organisational context Providing support Working relationships	Acting assertively

Building teams

Communicating

Influencing others |
| C4.3 Minimise conflict in your team | | |
| D1.1 Gather required information | D1.1 and D1.2 Analytical techniques Communication Information handling Organisational context | Managing self

Searching for information |
| D1.2 Inform and advise others | | Thinking and taking decisions |

Case studies

Below are two case studies that could be used as staff-meeting discussion points. Talk about what you would do and why you would do it. Consider what policies and procedures you would use to support your decision and why.

You have recently become a childminder and have joined the local childminding group. You have just completed the Developing Childminding Certificate and are full of new ideas that you want to try out. The group meets in a small hall with one small sink. You notice that the group hardly ever has messy play, even though the majority of children are aged between eighteen months and two and a half years. You raise the idea of changing the layout of the hall to make messy play possible. The most experienced childminder is very dismissive, saying, 'We have tried that before and it won't work'. What do you do? Why?

Things to consider:

➤ the most experienced childminder's rationale for dismissing you – is she fearful of change, does she think that you will take on a more powerful role, does she feel threatened by you, could it be that she is lazy and is just trying to avoid clearing up a mess?
➤ ways of getting the other team members to support you – who are your allies in your group?
➤ the benefits to the children
➤ small steps towards your aims, that may get you there eventually.

When you came to the setting, you implemented a new planning system, against much opposition. A few months later, the staff are complaining that this new system is too cumbersome and that the planning sheets take too long to complete. You decide to use the staff meeting to introduce your ideas for improving the system.

However, you are aware that some staff will want to say, 'I told you so', and there are other staff who do not want to plan at all and will use any excuse to avoid doing it. You recognise that although the system needs improvement, it has brought order and balance to how the curriculum is implemented. How will you introduce the change to your colleagues?

Things to consider:

➤ how you must present yourself throughout the meeting
➤ what you must know
➤ what information you will share with the staff and why
➤ what the possible dynamics in the group are
➤ how you will take the idea forward.

Chapter 5 Managing conflict

> ➤ **Reducing the chances of conflict**
> ➤ **Skills needed to deal with conflict**
> ➤ **Reacting to problems**
> ➤ **Problem-solving and negotiation**
> ➤ **Responding to conflict at work**
> ➤ **Useful policies for dealing with conflict**
> ➤ **Managing stress**

Managing conflict is probably the least favourite role for many managers; however, it is an inevitable part of managerial life. Conflict is stressful and unpleasant but best dealt with quickly and efficiently as it rarely resolves itself.

The image conjured up of 'managing conflict' is that of an aggressive, angry, rude adult (parent, professional staff member or visitor) demanding and complaining about some aspect of the service. This can be true and, increasingly, managers have to deal with very unpleasant adults. However, conflict also includes:

➤ dealing with demotivated staff
➤ opening closed minds
➤ responding to staff who have a negative attitude
➤ responding to staff who do not do their work and cause an atmosphere that affects other staff
➤ dealing with staff who have difficulty accepting their role and responsibility.

Dealing with any form of conflict is complicated and generally requires a two-pronged response. The first is to use effective problem-solving and decision-making techniques. The second is to create a non-threatening, risk-taking environment with effective policies and procedures, such as complaints procedures and disciplinary and grievance policies to help you respond when necessary.

Reducing the chances of conflict

Create a positive atmosphere
You can reduce the likelihood of problems arising by creating an atmosphere in which people feel appreciated and believe themselves to be an essential part of the organisation. Staff need to be encouraged to consider themselves as excellent reflective practitioners, and managers need to continually take every opportunity to generate excitement over what staff have achieved and what challenges must be met for the future. Ensure that you give new ideas careful thought and consideration, and give prompt, fair, accurate and reasoned feedback when ideas are rejected. Be clear about what is going to happen to the information offered and have a central 'Good ideas' book to save good ideas for the right time.

Create a non-blame environment
Generate a positive atmosphere in which creative ideas can flourish and demotivating boredom is reduced, by encouraging staff to be open and responsive

Manager's tip

Work hard to create a happy and respectful work environment. Involve your staff in specific tasks and celebrate their achievements. Provide nice snacks at meetings or offer little treats at other times.

and by respecting and using their spontaneity and originality. Create an organisational ethos based on continual improvement, where risk-taking is allowed and mistakes, where possible, are treated as learning experiences. Avoid a blame culture. Instead, keep the atmosphere positive so that the staff feel more able to be open to new ideas. Create a culture of continuous improvement where staff members reflect and learn from each other. Praise your staff both orally and in writing, letting them know how their ideas are to be used, and continually motivate them.

Deal with office politics and 'the grapevine'

All work places where people work together have 'politics'. The negative side of these office politics surfaces when individuals try to use it to increase their personal power, at the expense of colleagues and the organisation. As a manager, you need to create an environment in which status and hierarchy have as little importance as possible – this should limit the effects of 'politics'. Aim to treat people with respect, talk to them, be visible and approachable, and keep them well informed and up to date.

Know how change will trigger conflict

Change is good for raising achievement but it has to be dealt with sensitively and positively. Staff must be kept informed and involved. If they are not aware of the reasons for change they may respond defensively, be confrontational and create a very unpleasant atmosphere. Usually, this is because they are worried that changes mean more work and they may not be able to do it. Their fear of failure may be quite rational as they may be anxious that their lack of competence may be judged against them and they will lose face, status, reputation or ultimately their jobs (see Chapter 4).

Understand group dynamics

Group dynamics is concerned with the way groups function. Groups are 'live' and go through different phases, according to Tuckman (1965) (see below). This is a dynamic process and the stages do not always follow through. For example, a team may be 'norming', but when a new staff member joins, the team will reform and start through the process again. You must recognise the phases and understand how to respond.

Forming Testing times while the staff members get to know each other. They are finding out what the rules and expectations are and what behaviour will be accepted.

Storming Conflict begins to emerge between sub-groups. Power struggles emerge especially, as the leader starts to use their authority.

Norming The group starts to harmonise and gel. Conflicts are reconciled and resistance is overcome. Mutual support emerges.

Performing The group starts to perform, all working towards a common goal. It is a constructive time and the group energy is focused and purposeful. This phase, handled well, will lead to a high-performance team.

Dorming The group structure becomes governed by routine and systems, and is very closed and cosy. The group is self-satisfied and no longer wants to set or meet challenges, relying instead on past achievements.

Skills needed to deal with conflict

The manager who is confident at solving problems, negotiating and making decisions is more likely to manage conflict, because the whole process requires these skills. Managers need to be effective at solving problems. Staff do not like managers who ignore problems or fail to negotiate and make decisions. Staff are often heard to criticise their managers because they could not or would not take a decision, leaving the staff feeling unsafe, unclear and without guidance. It is quite interesting that staff will be more supportive of a manager who makes wrong decisions than one who shirks their responsibility for making decisions and carrying them through. The decision-making approach, when it is used to deal with conflict, will follow the usual decision process but will be affected by the atmosphere and the authority of the manager. It needs careful consideration as to when, how and who will make the necessary decisions.

Making a decision

There are different styles of decision-making: autocratic, persuasive, consultative and consensus (see page 13). As a manager, you need to know when and why to use each one.

When dealing with conflict, be very aware of how the stage has been set. Do not walk into a more difficult situation. Think about the style that you will adopt and why, and use your negotiation skills to help you identify mutually acceptable decisions and to agree on the future action.

Key principles of decision-making

To make a decision, consider the following:

1 Identify the problem. Do not rush to try to solve the problem at this stage, and really consider the problem rather than the answer.
2 Gather key information, facts and opinions. Be aware of who will be affected by your decision. If you do not have relevant power to make a decision, contact those who do and ask for their input. Even if your manager does not need to sanction your decision, getting their advice is a good move. Keep the relevant people informed.
3 Look at the alternatives while taking into account the criteria that needs to be met. Avoid rushing an important decision just because others expect it.
4 Analyse the information against the long- and short-term impact. Look at where you are and decide where you want to be.
5 Choose what to do. Once a decision is clear, make it quickly rather than slowly.
6 Act on your decision and make sure that everyone knows about it.
7 Implement your decision.
8 Monitor the implementation of your decision.

Decisions are best made near to the information point rather than referred up through the hierarchy. This helps to keep communication open and frank and reduces confusion, misinterpretation and complete distortion. It is helpful if staff feel that their ideas are considered, irrespective of their role in the organisation. Indeed, it is helpful to encourage some conflict, competition and open debate on the grounds that the decision is of benefit to the whole organisation. However, managers must be ready to address this constructively.

Manager's tip
When deciding who should make a decision, the general rule of thumb is that those closest to the problem are in the best position to do something about it.

Before implementing a decision, remember the importance of using your negotiation skills. You need to ensure that you can persuade the staff members to agree to a successful outcome without loss of face and in a way that makes them feel that they have been involved fairly in all aspects of the decision-making.

Negotiations

➤ involve people
➤ always have an element of conflict running through them, so you need to use compromise and bargaining techniques to move the discussion forward
➤ are best carried out face to face
➤ resolve the issue for the future
➤ imply reaching a joint decision.

Implementation

Apart from the obvious consideration of practicability, whether or not a decision is effectively implemented depends on a clearly defined and communicated set of action points, with details of who is responsible for each stage of implementation and monitoring progress. Making the decision is often the easy bit; implementing is far more tricky because it depends on the support and trust of your staff. Successful implementation is more likely if you:

➤ determine who will do what by when (action plan)
➤ share the action plan with everyone concerned
➤ establish a review procedure
➤ ensure that the reviews take place.

Remember that decisions that tackle only one part of a problem tend to fail. For example, you may remove a member of staff who is rude and aggressive but if the problem is due to poor management or an insufficient recruitment procedure, then nothing has been really resolved.

Reacting to problems

A problem can be dealt with in the following ways:

Tackle it yourself
Find out, think about it, define the issue, then make a decision.

Pass it on
Do you have to deal with the problem just because you have identified it? Perhaps another department, for example, personnel or finance, may be better at dealing with it. Indeed, you may aggravate the situation by dealing with it yourself, and taking away the problem may cause resentment. Help the person closest to the problem to solve it.

Take advice
'A problem shared is a problem halved', so, where appropriate, seek advice from colleagues and specialists.

Set up a working party

The issue may raise a more fundamental problem that may need long-term consideration. Get together a task force of people with different skills, experience and perspectives to deal with complex problems and identify strategies for action. However, sometimes task forces get things out of proportion, so keep yours focused. The group should be small and given a time target to make recommendations as well as adequate time to think. You require a reasoned and rational decision, not the response of a harassed group squeezing in another task before lunch.

Seek the advice of a consultant

If you seek the advice of a consultant, make sure that the terms of reference are very well thought out. You may wish the consultant to help you find a resolution to a problem that you have already defined or, alternatively, you may want the consultant to define the problem and the options available to you.

Ignore it

This can be a dangerous strategy as problems tend to get worse when not tackled. Occasionally, however, letting a problem resolve itself is a wise policy.

Problem-solving and negotiation

The problem-solving process

1 Define the problem.
2 Specify a range of solutions.
3 Consider all the available resources.
4 Evaluate the alternatives.
5 Make a judgement about the best option.
6 Select the best option.
7 Check the understanding of those involved in implementing the decision. Are they clear about what to do?
8 Implement the decision.
9 Monitor the implementation of the decision.
10 Draw up a check-list.

The process of negotiation

➤ Put yourself in the other person's shoes and seek common ground.
➤ Empathise with the other person and avoid blaming them for the problem.
➤ See both sides of the problem, discuss them and build bridges.
➤ Recognise and understand your emotions and the other person's.
➤ Allow time to let off steam.
➤ React calmly to emotional outbursts.
➤ Be ready to compromise.
➤ Communicate clearly and check the other person's understanding.
➤ Be open and share information.
➤ Build relationships and avoid stalemate.

Responding to conflict at work

Conflict is inevitable when people interact at work. Be brave, logical and positive, and deal with the situation quickly. Conflict is a behaviour that has been provoked by a situation or series of actions. It is a response to a problem. It may not be the best way to respond or you may not share the reason for the anger, but if you are the manager it needs to be resolved to limit the effects and consequences of the conflict.

Review the policies and procedures that you have available to deal with conflict. Check who is available to help you decide what to do. If you are a childminder, you may want to talk to another childminder or seek advice from your local Childminding Association, the NCMA or the OFSTED helpline.

Keep calm and think the process through very logically. You must be sure what you want to happen, even if in the end the outcome is different from what you wanted. Remain in control. Diffuse the situation where possible and find a compromise. Avoid a win–lose situation by finding a middle way.

The aggressive adult

Use the following strategies to deal with aggressive adults in the work place:

➤ Treat people with dignity and respect.

➤ Build relationships – you will maximise the chance of conflict management. It takes time, but it is well spent because it is a good basis for success.

➤ Do not be afraid and use all the known techniques to keep everyone calm.

➤ Put yourself in their shoes and think about what would calm them. Listen to them, then ask questions. Let conflicts come to the surface.

➤ Learn to communicate and to recognise the different ways in which we communicate as this is the basis of any good relationship. Learn to read between the lines and see what the real issue at stake is. Learn to listen, clarify and confirm. Read body language and connect with the feelings being expressed. Be sensitive to your own discomfort, tuning into times when you feel uncomfortable or when the signs are not right. Understand the importance of personal space and tone of voice.

➤ Become competent in creating dialogues and opening communication instead of shutting it down. Learn how to respond to and acknowledge others' feelings by getting in touch with your own. Recognise your own attitudes and how they might be impacting on progress. Do you sound more judgemental than you think? Try to see the other person's point of view.

➤ Aim to resolve the difficulty through negotiation and understanding. Find ways of letting people know that you are acknowledging, and are sensitive to, their feelings. Look at the issue from both perspectives and find a compromise.

➤ Be clear about your own values. Have a bottom line. When you are clear, you are less likely to sound defensive.

➤ Always have a set of core statements or prospectus with supporting policies and procedures to back your view.

➤ Use a problem-solving approach to conflicts. Be flexible and negotiate. Ask yourself how willing you are to really solve the problem.

➤ Commit yourself to lifelong learning. It is sometimes lack of understanding and information that keeps a conflict alive.

➤ The best outcome is that each person comes to view the issue from the other's perspective, having been sensitive and respectful throughout that process.

Conducting a meeting to raise issues of conflict

The following tips will help all parties to talk about issues of conflict in a calm manner:

➤ Make the room comfortable and safe. Arrange the furniture so that you are facing each other but on an equal level – do not sit behind your desk.

➤ Prepare for the meeting. Have the relevant evidence with you so that you do not fumble and seem confused during the discussion.

➤ Open the meeting calmly and clearly. Explain what you want to talk about and how long the meeting will last. Be open about its purpose and state clearly that you are aiming for a positive outcome. However, do not decide in advance what outcome you want. There may be a need to compromise.

➤ Let everyone have their say.

➤ Use active listening and appropriate body language to facilitate two-way communication. Adapt your approach to unexpected responses.

➤ Balance talking and listening. Hear what people are saying even if you do not like it or do not agree. Allow the person to explain their behaviour or performance and to suggest mitigating circumstances.

➤ Use the facts and evidence to support your input.

➤ Encourage the person to suggest solutions and a way forward.

➤ Consider in advance what support you could offer to assist the person to improve their performance or conduct.

➤ Think about the whole team and how you will support them, and rebuild the team when the conflict has been resolved.

➤ Agree a review period for future performance and conduct, and make clear the consequences for a lack of improvement or repeat behaviour.

➤ Make a written record of the meeting and give the person a copy. Ask them to sign it, as proof that they agree that it is a fair recording of the meeting and of the outcome.

Points for consideration

➤ Aggressive behaviour in the work place may disguise personal difficulties – avoid jumping to conclusions and listen.

➤ Take time to talk to staff members that come to see you.

➤ Never take sides in a staff quarrel. Be impartial.

➤ Find the root cause of the problem.

➤ Never give in to unreasonable demands. Compromise.

➤ Always rebuild your team after conflict.

Useful policies for dealing with conflict

Parents' complaints procedure

Encourage parents who feel unhappy with any aspect of your setting to discuss their concerns with the staff immediately. In order for the complaint to be dealt with effectively, have a complaints procedure, which could follow this format:

1 The parent needs to make an appointment to discuss the matter with the child's key worker. At this stage, the intention is to resolve the situation.

2 If the situation cannot be resolved, the parent needs to ask to see the manager or supervisor, who will have to arrange a meeting within three working days.
3 In the unlikely situation that the matter cannot be resolved between the manager and parent, the manager may have access to a senior manager, such as a regional manager, development manager or head teacher. He or she should have considered a procedure regarding this meeting, for example, seeing the parent within five working days of referral.
4 If the situation cannot be resolved at this level, a further stage may be built into the procedure, for example, a referral to the management committee or board of trustees. The manager should make sure that this body can make the final decision.

Parents have a right to complain to OFSTED and it is recommended that you display the OFSTED complaints department telephone number.

The finer points of a procedure can be written to meet the needs of your setting. The key objective is to have a procedure in place and to make sure that your staff know how to use it and that parents have been given a copy as part of their information pack.

The disciplinary procedure

The disciplinary policy is very useful to deal with poor performance, which may include conflict and negative attitude. The policy often has a positive effect and can be used to help someone back on track. It gives a clear message to the staff member that you are not prepared to tolerate a certain behaviour, which is demotivating for you and the team and causing bad feeling. It also gives the rest of the team the message that you are not afraid to deal with conflict.

Before applying the policy, read it carefully. The policy procedures must be followed correctly if the disciplinary is to succeed. You do not want to fall at the last hurdle because you have made one procedural mistake. Disciplinary policies usually cover the issues of capability (ability to do the job) and conduct (the way that one behaves while working both inside and outside the building). The policy will also include a definition of gross misconduct, which is an action that effectively breaks the contract of employment, allowing the employer, having established the facts and conducted a disciplinary hearing, to dismiss the member of staff without notice.

Examples of gross misconduct include theft, serious breach of health and safety standards, child abuse and threatened or actual bodily harm.

However, there may be other situations particular to your organisation that constitute gross misconduct, including:

➤ smoking in front of the children
➤ sexual relationships with a parent.

Make sure that all staff know what constitutes gross misconduct in the organisation and understand that any breaches will be treated as gross misconduct, which may lead to instant dismissal. You need to decide if a situation is about conduct or capability because the responses will differ accordingly. For example, if a staff member is observed swearing at a parent, you might consider this a conduct issue, but if you observe a staff member using inappropriate language with the children, you may decide that it is a capability issue because they have had no guidance on the subject. Some issues, particularly about attitude, concern both capability and conduct.

Disciplinary policies usually identify courses for action with specific procedures for each. Generally they are:

1 oral warning
2 written warning
3 final warning
4 specific guidance for gross misconduct, which may jump all three previous steps and include suspension.

It is not necessary to go through each stage. The situation may be sufficiently serious for you to immediately consider applying stage two or three. Whatever the situation, you have a duty to investigate and identify the reasons for the behaviour. It may be due to poor leadership or personal issues. The result of the investigation will determine the next steps. However, failure by the employer to investigate properly may lead to a claim by the staff member of harassment or unfair dismissal.

If the staff member is found guilty of unacceptable conduct

If the investigation finds the staff member guilty of unacceptable conduct, the manager will need to arrange a disciplinary hearing (following the policy to the letter). The result of the hearing will determine what action to take, for example:

➤ The evidence may indicate that there is no case to answer and so the staff member will continue working with no disciplinary record.
➤ The member of staff was at fault but did not understand what they were doing wrong. Perhaps they had received no supervision and did not realise the impact of their conduct. You could remedy this problem by providing relevant training and by checking their continued understanding and application within their practice.
➤ You issue an oral warning identifying the problem and the consequences of a failure to improve. You have a duty to give the staff member reasonable time to improve. You could support this process by training, coaching or increased supervision.
➤ You issue a written warning on the basis that there were mitigating circumstances, such as provocation. This warning will remain on the person's file for six months and be accompanied by clear explanation of the consequences of any repeat of such behaviour.
➤ Dismissal.

Summary action points

1 You need to conduct an investigation.
2 If you suspend a staff member you must continue to pay them until they return to work or are dismissed.
3 If you are in any way involved in the problem, arrange for someone else to conduct the investigation.
4 Written statements need to be taken from witnesses.
5 Everything relevant to the situation needs to be examined and recorded.
6 If you were the person delegated to conduct the hearing through the disciplinary procedure, have a colleague help you to decide the verdict and response.
7 Have all the relevant facts been gathered for the disciplinary hearing? Did the member of staff know about the complaint before the hearing to allow them to prepare properly? Do they know that they have a right to be accompanied and that a witness can attend the hearing and take notes?

Remember
If you dismiss the staff member and they go to an industrial court, the case will fail if the investigation and the hearing have not been completed thoroughly.

The grievance procedure
Grievance procedures must not be confused with disciplinary procedures. A grievance is when a member of staff is upset by their treatment either by another colleague or by their manager. If this happens, however unreasonably, the member of staff has the right to have their problem heard. Indeed, under the Employment Rights Act 1996, there must be a grievance procedure in place so that members of staff know how to deal with any issues that may arise. Grievance can be about anything, although they tend to be concerned with colleague conflict, management decisions, harassment, workload, poor health and safety, or salary discrepancies. A grievance that remains unresolved could result in an industrial tribunal.

If a member of staff brings a grievance, there is implied conflict. Therefore the matter needs to be handled carefully so that the outcome will be satisfactory and relationships left undamaged. A badly handled grievance may lead to:

➤ loss of a good staff member
➤ disciplinary problems and an increase in conflict
➤ wider problems across the organisation, involving more staff
➤ complaints to an employment tribunal
➤ poor performance, demotivation and unpleasant working environment
➤ unhealthy stress.

The grievance procedure, like the disciplinary procedure, has stages of action:

➤ The first stage will try to offer the staff ways of resolving the issue through informal discussion.
➤ The second stage will include a written formal complaint to a senior manager. Usually a decision is made at this stage.
➤ If the complainant is not happy with the decision, they may be able to access a further stage, which involves the trustees, management committee or governors.

The emphasis must be on the staff member knowing the process and their rights and responsibilities. Usually, the decision of the hearing is final and both parties are given it in writing. However, if it is found that the grievance is about a breach in the contract of employment or race, sex or disability discrimination, it could be referred to an employment tribunal. Under the Employment Bill 2002 an employer who fails to follow a fair procedure in dealing with an employee's grievance, or in the way that an employee is disciplined, will find that the compensation awarded by the tribunal can be significantly increased.

Whistle-blowing
Members of staff owe their employers a duty of loyalty, confidentiality and good faith. This means that they should have the best interests of their employer at heart. If they see another member of staff acting in a dishonest or irregular way, they should be encouraged to disclose it, rather than collude by covering it up. In early years settings this may mean reporting someone who is unkind or harsh with the children.

Disclosing behaviour is very hard to do and members of staff usually try to sort matters out at a local level. This may mean keeping the children away from the individual staff member, double-checking someone's work or intervening, as subtly as possible, to achieve a positive outcome.

However, staff need proper channels to disclose their concerns. They must also feel that any complaints or concerns will be taken seriously. Equally, they must be aware that malicious allegations will be treated as gross misconduct. There is now statutory protection for 'whistle-blowers' after decades of fear of reprisals.

The Public Interest Disclosure Act 1998 is designed to protect staff from dismissal or punishment should they reveal information that they reasonably believe exposes such matters as financial malpractice, miscarriages of justice, danger to health and safety, abuses of care and risks to the environment. The Act covers both the public and private sectors.

In order to gain special statutory protection, the disclosure in question must be through one of the six specified procedures:

1 A criminal offence has taken place or is likely to take place.

2 There has been or is likely to be a failure to comply with legal obligations.

3 There has been or is likely to be a miscarriage of justice.

4 The environment has been or is likely to be damaged.

5 The health and safety of any individual has been or is likely to be endangered.

6 Information tending to show any of the above has been or is likely to be concealed.

Disclosure procedures

Even if the disclosure meets any of the above criteria, it must be made known in the correct way, or the statutory protection will be lost. The correct procedure is disclosure by a member of staff:

➤ in good faith to the employer or responsible person

➤ to a legal advisor in the course of obtaining legal advice

➤ in good faith to a Government minister, where the worker's employer is a public servant or body directly appointed by the state

➤ to a prescribed person such as a health and safety officer in good faith

➤ to other external sources, not listed above, where the member of staff feels that they will be victimised by their employer, or that the evidence will be concealed or destroyed. The disclosure must be made in good faith and not for personal gain.

Under the 1998 Act it is automatically unfair to dismiss a member of staff because they have made a protected disclosure, and they cannot be punished in other ways such as fines or demotion. All settings should have a 'whistle-blowing' policy and this should include information on:

➤ examples of the types of concern that staff should raise, such as abusive practices, fraud or corruption, unauthorised use of organisation funds and unethical conduct

➤ individuals who may use the employer's whistle-blowing policy

➤ channels of communication when raising concerns

➤ how to raise concerns

➤ circumstances of external disclosure

➤ action to be taken on receipt of a concern

➤ providing feedback to those who whistle-blow

➤ offering staff advice and support
➤ effective policy promotion.

Managing stress

Stress is an emotional response to life and life's challenges. There is positive and negative stress. Positive stress keeps us alive and encourages us to stretch ourselves and meet challenges. Negative stress makes us feel overwhelmed to such a degree that it affects our health. Symptoms such as sleeplessness and difficulty in getting to sleep, fidgeting, dizzy spells, nausea, irritability, and difficulty in relaxing and concentrating, are associated with stress, although these are also symptoms of a range of minor and major ailments. Conflict can cause negative stress as well.

Response to stress varies in individuals and many factors, including our childhood, adolescence and life experiences, are significant influences. Each member of your staff will also respond differently to conflict and other demands made by work. Good management requires that you develop an emotional intelligence so that you become aware of how someone else is feeling and adjust your own behaviour to respond accordingly.

Stress-reducing systems

Consider the following:

➤ Do all your staff know how they contribute to the organisation?
➤ Are they clear about what is expected of them?
➤ Do they have some element of control? (Lack of control is a key cause of stress.)
➤ Can they contribute to operational and long-term developments?
➤ Do you regularly load them down with tasks and call it 'delegation'?
➤ Can they negotiate time targets?
➤ Do you ensure that staff can make decisions that you support?
➤ Have you got a good recruitment, induction and training programme to help staff meet their potential?
➤ Are your staff helped to take responsibility for managing their own stress? Stress is not just a problem to be blamed on the organisation – staff need to take responsibility for their well-being too. Aim to provide a range of support programmes such as yoga classes, health advice or massage sessions, and try to help staff keep a balance between their lives and their work. It is everyone's responsibility to create a supportive and healthy work place for the benefit of the children.

Stress-reduction check-list

➤ Look after yourself.
➤ Start the day relaxed.
➤ Make sure that you eat breakfast.
➤ Keep a check on caffeine and alcohol levels. Self-prescribed drugs do not always help.
➤ Do not rush around trying to do too many things at once. Organise and prioritise. You do not have to say 'yes' to everyone and everything.
➤ Learn to recognise the signs of stress. Do not wait until you are in crisis before you seek help.
➤ Identify what stresses you. Change what you can and work realistically with what you cannot.

➤ Be assertive, say 'no' and take control in your working life. Do not say 'yes' if you mean 'no'.

➤ Identify achievable steps, then use a small-steps approach to achieve them.

➤ Check if you exercise enough and are eating the right foods.

➤ At work, take proper breaks. Go out to lunch occasionally.

➤ Healthy environments are important – check that your working conditions are satisfactory.

➤ Keep a sense of perspective. Do not try to be perfect and remember what you have done well.

➤ Being a manager demands a lot of you, so every now and then put yourself first. Protect your own time. Relaxation and leisure are not treats – they are essential.

➤ Talk about your problems and share them with your friends. Consider whether you need to change jobs.

Think about

Can you, really and all the time:

➤ use appropriate behaviour in stressful situations

➤ apply resilience in pressure situations

➤ remain effective in a range of working situations

➤ keep a balance between priorities

➤ take into account the level of stress in others?

NVQ in Management Level 3 links

Elements	Knowledge evidence	Personal competencies
C4.3 Minimise conflict in your team	C4.3 Information handling Organisational context Working relationships	Acting assertively Behaving ethically Building teams
D1.3 Hold meetings	D1.3 Communication Leadership styles Meetings Organisational context	Communicating Focusing on results Influencing others
C15.2 Contribute to implementing disciplinary and grievance procedures	C15.2 Disciplinary and grievance procedures Information handling Legal requirements Organisational context Working relationships	Managing self Searching for information Thinking and taking decisions

Case studies

Below are two case studies that could be used as staff-meeting discussion points. Talk about what you would do and why you would do it.

You have a new trainee member of staff. This is her first job and she seems eager to please. You have been giving her lots of praise and she has accessed quite a few training courses. However, you notice that recently she has been quite moody at times, making little eye contact, being quite brusque and especially sharp and intolerant with a certain member of staff. Staff are inclined to tiptoe around her and wait until she softens up. You are unhappy because it is causing tension and conflict in the room.

➤ What do you do?
➤ What policies will you use to help you?
➤ How do you respond to the other staff members?
➤ How will this reflect on the member of staff's future?

You are a new childminder and have been looking after Sally since she was six months old. Now at eleven months she has discovered the joys of painting and messy play. Her parents hate to see her grubby and are increasingly cross and difficult when they come to collect her. You are in a dilemma: Sally really enjoys messy play and you have recently been on training courses that confirmed the importance of such experiences. However, you are more and more worried by her parents' aggressive approach.

➤ What do you do and what outcome do you want?
➤ Where do you get support?

Useful information

Legislation relevant for this chapter
Disability Discrimination Act 1995; Employment Rights Act 1996; Care Standards Act 2000; The ACAS Code of Practice on Disciplinary and Grievance Procedures.

Publications
➤ Advisory, Conciliation and Arbitration Services (ACAS), Head Office, Brandon House, 180 Borough High Street, London SE1 1LW. National Helpline: 0845-747 4747. Website: www.acas.org.uk
  - *Discipline at Work* (handbook)
  - *Producing Disciplinary and Grievance Procedures* (guide)
➤ Department of Trade and Industry. DTI Enquiry Unit, 1 Victoria Street, London SW1H 0ET. Tel: 020-7215 5000. Website: www.dti.gov.uk
  - *Dismissal – Fair and Unfair: A Guide for Employers* (employment legislation)
  - *Unfairly Dismissed?* (employment legislation)

Chapter 6 Creating a safe environment

> ➤ **Health and Safety at Work etc Act 1974**
> ➤ **Care Standards Act 2000**
> ➤ **Health and safety policy**
> ➤ **Child protection policy**
> ➤ **Abuse against staff**
> ➤ **Key health and safety legislation**

Maintaining efficient health and safety for all staff and children throughout the day is a major task. Managers have the overall responsibility for health and safety at an early years setting, but every staff member also has an individual responsibility for maintaining their own health and safety and paying due care and attention to those of colleagues and visitors.

In most early years settings, a member of staff is given the role of Health and Safety Officer (HSO), which requires them to work with the manager to implement the policies, appropriately and effectively, and to keep abreast of the latest health and safety requirements and recommendations. This is a vital role and it is very important that HSOs have a proper induction and specific training. They are likely to be responsible for imparting new information to the staff team and this must be shared in a pragmatic way so that the issue comes alive and is immediately understood in relation to the law and how it has to be implemented in the setting.

Health and Safety at Work etc Act 1974

The basis of British health and safety law is the Health and Safety at Work etc Act 1974. The Act sets out the general duties that employers have towards their employees and members of the public, and that employees have to one another. The main aim of the Act is to raise safety standards, with particular emphasis on how the necessary work is organised, supervised and carried out. It places a major responsibility on you, the manager, to do 'all that is reasonably practicable' to ensure the health and safety of all people at work (including contractors such as window cleaners), those who might be affected by your activities (for example, visitors who may fall on your site) and the public. You must also provide a safe working environment and a competent body of staff.

The law places a duty of care on employers. This means that they must ensure that their employees are fit for work, and so that health screening and monitoring may be required.

The Act also states that employees have a duty of care to themselves and their colleagues, and must co-operate with their employers and any other person in order to enable them to perform the necessary duties imposed on them by safety legislation. Employers and employees are also required to comply with the Disability Discrimination Act 1995.

Employers have to meet a number of requirements, and failure to do so will result in prosecution, a fine of up to £20,000 or imprisonment. They must:

➤ publish a health and safety policy
➤ arrange to have health and safety officers
➤ establish a health and safety committee, which must meet four times a year, produce an agenda and circulate minutes
➤ appoint a competent person to assess and evaluate risks and hazards
➤ carry out risk assessments
➤ arrange protection from unavoidable risks
➤ provide safety training
➤ monitor and improve safety arrangements
➤ provide health-risk surveillance.

If there is a situation where the manager is found to be liable for failing to meet their responsibilities, the courts will not accept lack of funds and resources or ignorance as mitigating factors. It is worth remembering that employers can also be prosecuted for negligence under criminal or civil liability. In addition, employees who are negligent can be personally liable. However, the employer will also be liable if the negligence took place during the employee's duties. These duties are qualified in the Act by the principle 'so far as is reasonably practicable'.

What the law requires is that managers look at what the risks are and take sensible measures to tackle them. They need to conduct two risk assessments per year, record the findings and what action has been taken. Risk assessment should be simple and straightforward, and all staff should be able to read and understand the document.

In addition to carrying out risk assessment, employers need to:

➤ make arrangements for implementing the health and safety measures identified in the risk assessment
➤ take account of the needs of any young person (16 to 18 years), temporary workers, pregnant workers and new mothers in the work place
➤ appoint competent people to help them implement the arrangements, such as a health and safety officer
➤ set up emergency procedures and ensure that all staff understand what these are and what they should do
➤ provide clear information and training to staff
➤ work together with other employers sharing the same work place, such as an after-school club or playgroup sharing a school site.

The Health and Safety Executive and Commission are the operating arm of the law. They look at ways of helping people to put the law into practice and produce guidance, regulations and approved codes of practice to help employers know how to interpret the Act.

Care Standards Act 2000

The Care Standards Act 2000 lays down the required standards for all childcare settings. Every manager should have a good understanding of both the Act and the Guidance, and their copies should be well thumbed. The Guidance helps to translate the Standards into practice. For example, in the Standards for Full Daycare, Standard 7 is Health and the first criterion is 7.1: 'The premises and equipment are clean'. Page 33 of the Guidance describes this in terms of establishing a daily cleaning routine, a rota system for washing toys, dressing-up clothes and other equipment, liaising with cleaning services, providing hand-washing and hand-drying facilities and so on.

Integrate procedures into your routine

The routine needs to be designed to include opportunities for meeting such legal responsibilities in the work place. Managers need to feel assured that if an inspector called, he or she could see evidence of when and how the setting is cleaned, for example, that systems are in place for washing toys and how you have trained the staff about food hygiene, Control of Substances Hazardous to Health (COSHH), Hazard Analysis and Critical Control Points (HACCP) and Paediatric First Aid. Such evidence could be in the form of a rota sheet that everyone can see, COSHH notices displayed on bright laminated card in key areas of the setting, and so on.

Environmental services frequently conduct unannounced spot checks and check records, display information, fridges, food samples, staff-training records and any information that they require which shows that the setting is maintaining the necessary procedures for health and safety. Following the visit, they will send a report that may include specific requirements regarding health and safety.

Key documents

All your records must be up to date, correctly completed and reviewed annually to make sure that the relevant information is being collected. This will include:

➤ accident and incident forms
➤ administration of medicine procedures
➤ a contingency plan for evacuation. This is not just for fire but for other situations, particularly for settings in high-risk areas. It is more in-depth than a fire drill because the plan needs to include a map of the building, so that the emergency services can know where dangerous objects or a person could be hidden. The contingency plan also needs contact details of all children and staff and an agreed alternative meeting place in case the staff cannot re-enter the building for long periods.
➤ daily records of fridge temperature and food samples for each cooked meal, to be kept in the fridge for five days, in case a child gets salmonella poisoning (the sample will be checked by an environmental health officer to help trace the source in such a situation)
➤ fire drills with clear information about each drill
➤ health and safety meetings (four times a year, each with the records of the minutes)
➤ maintenance checks on the building and on portable appliances
➤ risk assessment (twice yearly)
➤ risk assessment for staff (pregnant staff, those with recurrent problems such as a bad back or those returning to work following serious illness).

Health and safety policy

Having a policy is a very effective way of managing health and safety in the setting. A health and safety policy is different from others in that it includes policies and procedures for all the key areas, including :

➤ contingency evacuation
➤ display screen equipment
➤ fire
➤ first aid regulations
➤ food hygiene
➤ manual handling
➤ personal safety and dealing with violence
➤ portable appliances
➤ protective clothing for cooks.

Writing a policy

Begin your policy with a statement that sets out what you want to achieve. It may read, 'The employer will make every effort to create a safe and healthy environment for all employees, children and anyone who works or attends the setting, and all reasonable steps will be taken to meet its health and safety responsibilities and to comply with all relevant legislation'. To ensure that your statement is valid, have it signed by the managing director, chief executive or whoever has overall responsibility for the setting (they carry the overall responsibility but designate the operational responsibility to you, the manager).

Get into the habit of building health and safety into annual plans and business plans. The law requires a health and safety policy but, to be effective, the policy also needs to concentrate on prevention and partnership with staff to promote health and well-being. The Chartered Institute of Personnel and Development (see page 16) believes that the effective management of health and welfare at work contributes to performance improvement, lowers the chances of staff resorting to litigation, reduces absenteeism and work-place illness and injuries, and improves morale.

The policy must include sections on how you will operate within health and safety procedures and legislation, how you will measure your performance and how you will use the findings to feed into the review process. Consider the following:

➤ Carry out pre-employment health checks to ensure that all staff are fit physically and mentally to work with children.
➤ Create a role for a health and safety officer. There needs to be a designated person to help you meet the responsibilities of health and safety. The whole team will need to know exactly what their role is and how each member of staff must respond to their requests and expectations. This is particularly important for managers who need to ensure that the policy is implemented and that everyone knows what is expected of them.
➤ Ensure that your staff induction system makes all staff (including temporary workers and students) aware of how and why they need to comply with health and safety procedures and policies.
➤ Undertake monitoring of children and staff accidents and incidents. Include 'near-misses' for assessment and recording within the Reporting of Injuries,

Diseases and Dangerous Occurrences Regulations 1995 (RIDDOR). This should be carried out every six months to check that there is not a pattern emerging in the accidents that may, in turn, identify poor surfaces or supervision or some unsafe equipment. When reporting accidents, you need two copies of the accident records of each child's accident: a copy for the parents and one for the setting. You must have a separate system for staff accidents. All accidents should be recorded in the HMSO-approved accident book.

➤ Complete health and safety risk assessments. This should take place twice a year and the resulting information must be dealt with appropriately.

➤ Explain to all staff how to ensure effective food hygiene. This includes HACCP using food probes.

➤ Ensure that there is a fire-drill system in place and a recording system to check the success of each drill. There will also need to be a regular system of checking all fire equipment.

➤ Ensure that first-aid procedures are in place. There must be a regular system for checking the contents of the first-aid box and where it is placed. You may need more than one box according to the size and shape of your building. All staff need to be confident about dealing with first-aid needs.

➤ Make sure that you have procedures for hygiene. These include nappy-changing, waste disposal and access to and expectations within the kitchen.

➤ Put in place arrangements for undertaking necessary repairs and maintenance work related to health and safety. This will need to include annual portable electrical appliances tests.

➤ Provide advice on a range of issues, including drugs, alcohol, HIV, AIDS and immunisation. The policy could include a statement about the setting's approach to staff and families with HIV, and guidance on immunisation especially for staff who work with babies.

➤ Carry out regular risk analysis of the premises and share information about the action taken to deal with hazardous situations. This includes procedures for RIDDOR which require managers to report certain categories of injury or disease sustained by people at work, including dangerous occurrences and gas incidents.

➤ Put together a set of procedures about access to the premises. This should cover who is allowed on the premises, who has keys and can lock up, who knows the burglar-alarm code and the number of staff who stay in the building after and before working hours.

➤ Regularly check the premises and know how to recognise a pest infestation and how to respond if necessary.

➤ Promote a good health education programme to help staff be healthy and fit. Some organisations put in place an occupational health programme. This is used to monitor the health of employees and promote health activities in line with legal requirements, including European Union directives.

➤ Keep the staff training programme up to date and inform your staff on health and safety to help them minimise

personal risks and injuries. Training is important and each setting needs to decide what they consider imperative. It is advisable for each staff member to have training on:

- administration of medicines including emergency treatment such as inhalers (and volumisers) and epinephrine auto-injectors
- COSSH
- fire drills
- food hygiene, including HACCP
- manual handling
- paediatric first aid
  In addition to these, managers and HSOs should also:
- comply with the First Aid at Work Regulations (if more than 20 employees are on site)
- be familiar with the Health and Safety at Work etc Act 1974
- complete a Risk Assessment Training
➤ Ensure that all records are maintained.

Managers must make sure that their staff realise their responsibility with regards to health and safety. It is not just the job of the health and safety officer to keep the building and the people safe – it is the job of every member of staff to be vigilant and aware. They must do everything that they can to prevent injury to themselves, their colleagues, the children in their care and others affected by their actions or omissions at work. Staff need to be encouraged to behave in a sensible way at all times to reduce potential risk and inform managers or relevant staff members when they see a hazard or a risk. Finally, they must always behave in a way that will not cause danger to themselves or affect the safety of the children in their care or other people.

Display screen equipment (DSE)

More and more early years staff are using computers as part of their work, with the children as well as for writing reports, accessing e-mail and the Internet, completing spreadsheets and entering data. Under the requirements of the Health and Safety at Work etc Act 1974, employers need to take all reasonable steps to ensure the health and safety of employees who work with display screen equipment (computers and all the equipment associated with them). This includes having procedures on how to use the computer correctly and safely, such as taking rest breaks, having eye tests and using the correct equipment and information. Each workstation must be assessed for risk and any appropriate action taken to remove or reduce the risk of injury and ensure that each new employee is made aware of and understands their responsibilities under the policy.

Managers need to be aware, and make their staff aware, of some of the negative consequences of working with DSE. These could include itchy skin reactions to static electricity and dry atmosphere around DSE workstations and repetitive strain injuries (RSI).

The policy must take account of all those using DSE and refer to those with specific needs, such as pregnant women and staff suffering with sight impairment or back problems. Managers need to ensure that workstations are fitted with the correct, ergonomically designed equipment, that ventilation, space and light are suitable and that all equipment is serviced and kept well maintained.

Fire prevention and fire regulations

Everyone is at risk from a potential fire and all early years settings need to have a policy that addresses fire prevention. It should include how staff will take precautions to prevent fire, to contain the spread of fire and evacuate premises safely if there is a fire. Every setting will need a fire plan that will comprise:

➤ fire equipment (location, checking systems and maintenance)

➤ fire exits (location, checking-for-obstruction procedure, maintenance and security)

➤ routine fire procedures (staff induction, fire-equipment maintenance and fire drills) and an evacuation plan

➤ assembling at a pre-selected assembly point (agreeing on at least two assembly points both written on the fire plan)

➤ fire practice (fire-drill procedure, records and monitoring)

➤ training (staff induction for evacuation and how and when to use the equipment)

➤ risk assessment to include all the information from fire drills, equipment-maintenance reports and staff training.

Lifting and handling

Staff who work with children will constantly be lifting, pulling, pushing and transferring heavy weights as part of their daily routine. This can place an enormous strain on their backs and is a frequent reason for staff absence in early years settings. It is advisable that all staff, especially those working with babies and toddlers, have information and training on how to lift and handle weight safely. This should be included as part of the regular risk assessments, checking that every member of staff knows what lifting and handling they will need to undertake. Managers should pay additional attention to high-risk staff, such as those with back or physical injuries and those who are pregnant.

Managers need to be informed about, and make their staff aware of, their responsibilities in relation to relevant legislation, including the Manual Handling Operations Regulations 1992. They need to identify the practical steps to reduce risk and ensure that safe lifting is part of the staff induction and student policies. Staff must also be made aware that they have responsibility to look after themselves and their colleagues and must not take unnecessary risks. They need to co-operate with other staff members to ensure compliance with the setting procedures.

The staff should organise the setting's space so that all equipment is accessible, and make sure that a system of safe storage is adhered to. For example, the shed is usually a real point of risk, bikes, trikes and heavy outdoor equipment often being placed precariously and liable to fall and hurt someone, or cause somebody a back injury when moving them around, because they are so badly stored.

Care must also be taken when picking up children, especially when they are upset and writhing around, as they can be very strong, making it hard to balance and centre their weight and so putting the worker's back at risk.

Finally, the staff should arrange chairs, tables, changing mats and so on so that they are well supported, stable and safe, and make sure that the setting's floor is not slippery and that there are no obstructions.

Protective clothing for cooks

This policy will include procedures about:

➤ the purchase of protective clothing
➤ the responsibility of the cook for keeping work clothing clean and in reasonable repair
➤ the type of clothes that can be worn
➤ additional protective clothing
➤ when and where kitchen clothes and shoes can be worn
➤ wearing jewellery in the kitchen
➤ head covering
➤ footwear.

Protecting children in the setting

In order to ensure that children are safe in an early years setting, potential employees must undergo certain checks as part of the recruitment process (see Chapter 2). As a manager, you need to verify that every effort is made to carry out safety checks on all staff.

As part of the recruitment process, make it your policy to check references carefully. Recent research showed that three quarters of all employers checked references and that the proportion was even higher in the public sector. Indeed, an Internal Revenue Service (IRS) employment review showed that six out of ten employers had failed to confirm an appointment because of an unfavourable reference. One of the main reasons that employers cite for rejecting candidates on the basis of poor references was that they were exaggerating or lying about their experience and achievements. In 2001, the Risk Advisory Group, one of Europe's leading independent investigations and intelligence consultancies, checked almost 900 curricula vitae on behalf of employers and found that inaccuracies had increased by more than 20 per cent compared to those checked in 2000.

Candidates intending to work with children will need to have a police check, through the Criminal Records Bureau (CRB). The Bureau was set up to ensure that unsafe people were not recruited to work with vulnerable people, including children. Their procedures provide a more thorough check of a candidate's suitability, accessing information not just from police records but other records as well. This process is called 'disclosure' and there are three types: basic, standard and enhanced. Most staff in childcare will be checked under the standard-disclosure procedures. That means information will be provided by the CRB on any 'spent' conviction, as specified within the Rehabilitation of Offenders Act 1974 (Exceptions) Order 1975.

Personal safety and handling violence

It is important that all settings address the issues of personal safety for their staff. Increasingly, incidents are reported involving aggressive behaviour from parents and other adults towards staff members, every step should be taken to protect staff.

As with all policies, introduce a statement that identifies your broad aim. This may include what you mean by 'personal safety', such as 'physical abuse directed towards any person on the premises, damage to their property, verbal abuse or threats, or an act of aggression that is any form of verbal, psychological, racial or sexual harassment'.

Your health and safety policy needs to state what you will do to reduce the chance of such risks and how you will respond if a member of staff does experience violence. That may include regular inspections of the building, giving staff training on dealing with violence, making links with the community police officer, installing burglar alarms, providing counselling and support and, where appropriate, allowing staff time off, on full pay, for legal advice to be sought and to attend court if legal proceedings are pursued. As with all other policies, it will be the responsibility of the most senior group or person to ensure that the policy is operational and regularly reviewed. The procedures need to include sections on:

➤ security in the building
➤ systems for checking who is entering and leaving the building
➤ rights to refuse entry
➤ when to call the police
➤ how to manage meetings with parents and carers
➤ working late
➤ management of the staff's personal details.

If the setting does home visits, you will need to identify another set of procedures for this. These may include:

➤ numbers and types of staff members approved to go on the visit
➤ times of visits
➤ sharing information about where you have gone
➤ if you go home, who to tell that you are safe.

In order to ensure that staff feel safe in the work environment, managers must address the possibility of an aggression occurring and have a strategy in place to either prevent or reduce the possibility of staff being hurt or frightened.
   Avert problems by:

➤ checking how your staff feel about the risk
➤ using the risk-assessment process to consider how to deal with such risk, checking points of vulnerability
➤ keeping good records of incidents or 'near-misses' so that you can use the information to create strategies
➤ ensuring that you staff record all incidents, including verbal abuse, not just what they consider to be 'major incidents'
➤ considering how to give people a clear message that aggression towards staff will not be tolerated
➤ having an emergency code, for example, saying, 'I need a red file now', to mean 'Come to the office now, I need help'
➤ providing your staff with personal safety alarms
➤ training staff to prevent, defuse, respond and cope with violence or aggression.

Mental health at work
Managers who wish to create a healthy work place will need to recognise the need to establish policies and procedures in the area of mental health. The Health and Safety Executive (HSE) states that a mental health policy should be an integral part

of the setting's health and safety policy. In this way it gives a clear message that the employer is interested in the mental welfare of the staff. This is quite an important message considering that one in four people will experience some form of mental illness during the course of a year. Managers therefore are advised to ensure that the work-place environment is as safe and healthy as possible to reduce work-aggravated illness.

People with mental ill health continue to suffer discrimination at work. Under the Disability Discrimination Act 1995 it is unlawful for an employer to treat an employee with a disability more unfavourably. Mental illness is covered by the Act when it is 'recognised by a respected body of medical opinion' and has a substantial and long-term effect on the person's ability to carry out routine work.

Including a statement about mental health in your equal opportunities policy, identifying ways of reducing the barriers to employment within the organisation, is a positive start. In addition, you could provide training on disability awareness as well as ways of recognising when staff are becoming very vulnerable.

Managers need to create an environment where all employees are supported to develop and use their skills and potential. There need to be good systems in place to track issues such as absenteeism, increased staff turnover, high levels of tiredness and demotivation. Negative, unmanaged stress will build up if these issues are not addressed and may lead to mental ill health in staff.

Have good management practices in place, including:

➤ effective communication
➤ positive and open management
➤ encouraging a healthy balance between work and life
➤ consulting and involving the work-force.

These are all good ways to create a safe and healthy environment where staff are more likely to deal with stress and challenges healthily. See Chapter 5 for other measures to reduce stress.

The Health and Safety Executive recommends that occupational stress should be recognised as a health and safety issue, and a systematic problem-solving approach should be adopted to reduce negative stress within the setting.

If a staff member has mental health problems, you may need to make adjustments to support them, in line with your equal opportunities and health and safety policies. In addition, the reviewing process of these policies must be carried out by a working group that represents the work-force, who must act on their findings to create an open and anti-discriminatory environment which brings out the best in people.

Reviewing your policy

You do not need to review your health and safety policy more than once a year, unless an external event requires an immediate modification, for example, a change in the law and regulations, which impacts on the organisation's responsibility for health and safety.

If some changes are necessary but you need confirmation before taking action, ensure that all your staff as well as parents and carers are aware of the changes. It is a statutory duty to publish a health and safety policy and to make sure that it is complied with.

Child protection policy

The Children Act 1989 enshrines the principle that the welfare of the child is paramount. All early years settings are required to have a child protection policy to help ensure that, where possible, children are protected. Keeping children safe is a complex process involving co-operative work between a number of agencies. However, it is the Local Education Authorities that hold the statutory duty to investigate any situation where they have reasonable cause to suspect that a child 'is suffering or likely to suffer significant harm'.

Writing a child protection policy

It is advisable for early years settings to write their policies in conjunction with the Local Authority multi-agency guidelines. This means that the policy will include information about everyone's responsibility for protecting children and will reference inter-agency co-operation in both the planning and providing of services for a child and their family. However, policies and procedures alone cannot protect a child, but they can provide a good basis for sound practice and balanced sensitive judgement.

Every policy needs a clear aim, and a child protection policy will need to include what the setting will do to safeguard the welfare of the children, for example:

➤ working openly and honestly with parents and carers
➤ providing staff training and support
➤ making efforts to always work in collaboration with the statutory services
➤ reviewing the policy regularly.

The policy may need to include information about what you mean by 'child protection' so that staff are aware of the sorts of circumstances which would require action. It could be about child abuse and the legal definition as a useful basis for action. However, staff must be trained to treat each case separately and to avoid jumping to conclusions. This is the definition from the Children Act 1989: 'A child is considered to be in need of protection when the basic needs of that child are not being met through avoidable acts of either commission or omission'. These acts will usually be committed by parents, other carers or members of the household. However, any definition must contain three essential elements:

1 avoidable action by the adults in the household
2 demonstrable harm or potential harm to the child
3 a causal link between the first two elements.

How to make a referral

The child protection policy must include the procedures for making a referral. These will differ according to the setting and the service provided by the Local Authority. However, managing a child protection issue is very stressful, so all staff need very clear guidelines to help them make a referral. As the manager, you may be on leave and unable to support them, so it is important that everyone is clear about what to do.

Ensure that your staff have been trained to write the facts, not opinions, and how to use specific terms rather than general comments, for example, 'Child looks neglected'. Dealing with a child protection situation is worrying for all staff but many say that the most difficult part is knowing how to involve the parents or carers. It is generally much better to talk to them from the outset. If you are worried, the Social Services Department (SSD) will advise as to the best way to involve the parents. Early years staff usually want to maintain a positive relationship with the parents for the benefit of the child, who may continue attending the setting while there is an investigation. The one situation where staff are advised never to inform parents is where they suspect a case of sexual abuse. They must speak to the SSD beforehand.

It is wise to include a reference to child protection in the child's admission form and the terms and conditions of the setting. Have a statement that says that all early years staff have a duty to report any situation where they think that a child may be at risk of harm and will contact the SSD if necessary.

Some child protection situations dealt with by early years staff could be described as non-urgent and are usually known as chronic neglect. Staff need clear procedures about how to record and monitor such situations and where and when

to share the information. There is always a possibility of this escalating, so remember that it is the job of the SSD to decide if the matter is a child protection situation. If you are worried about the child, make the referral.

Include a section in your child protection policy about what to do if you suspect child sexual abuse. The procedures for this will differ, particularly with regards to collecting and sharing information, but there are three stages of initial intervention:

1 preliminary assessment
2 interview
3 medical examination.

Each intervention requires extreme sensitivity and competence in how to assess whether the child has experienced sexual abuse and to determine the necessary action needed to protect the child, maintain confidentiality appropriately and involve the parents in the process.

It is probably quite sensible to put in your policy what happens when you make a referral. Create a form where to collate all the information that will be needed by the referrer. It is recommended to seek the advice of the social work team when writing the policy because you are more likely to include relevant information that will make the process smoother for all concerned.

Remember that all child protection referrals require immediate attention and consideration by the duty social worker or manager to decide on actions and timing. The timing of the investigation will depend on the nature of the abuse and the seriousness of the allegations or injury, but they will try to achieve a balance between ensuring the safety of the child and organising a well-planned investigation. The policy needs to include the possible responses that a social worker may make following a referral. This information should be included in the policy, either as a section or an appendix. There should be information about:

➤ the child protection investigation
➤ an emergency situation
➤ the strategy meeting
➤ the child protection register and the criteria for a case of abuse
➤ the purpose of a case conference if invited to one.

You may also attach some information identifying legal references, including:

➤ emergency action
➤ assessment orders
➤ care proceedings.

Dealing with child protection can be a very upsetting situation, so the policy should include information about what internal support systems are in place to help staff who have to invoke the child protection procedures and who may have to continue to work with the family throughout an investigation.

Abuse against staff

While all early years settings need to have a child protection policy to help towards the safe keeping of children, it is also becoming advisable that managers consider writing an 'allegations of abuse against staff' policy. There is now a climate of increasing hostility and litigation, and staff are facing more aggression from adults. Having a policy would help your staff to know how to respond if a parent or another staff member made an allegation suggesting that they were hurting or had hurt a child. The policy would also need to address what would happen if an allegation was made about agency staff or a student.

In writing such a policy, the staff would need to decide what constitutes an allegation of abuse and clarify the difference between an allegation and a complaint, for example, when a staff member shouts or is impatient with the child but does not or has not hurt them.

As with all policies, you need to state what to do (including if the child is hurt), who to tell, when to tell and what to record. This is a very sensitive issue because the welfare of the child is paramount but, at the same time, the staff member is innocent until proven guilty and while that process is under way their reputation is at stake.

Likely responses

As a consequence of the allegation being made, a number of responses may occur, including a referral to the Social Services Department under the child protection procedures or to the police. If the allegation is more about inappropriate behaviour, it may need to be dealt with under your own disciplinary procedures. The allegation may be made as a result of a staff member taking a necessary course of action to prevent the child from being severely harmed or injured, and this action will be explained to the parents or carers under normal operational procedures. Every setting has to inform OFSTED if there is an allegation of abuse made about a staff member. Some settings may have contractual obligations that require them to inform the contractors if such a situation occurs.

Your child protection policy needs to explain possible situations, such as the requirement to attend a strategy meeting. For example, if a parent makes an allegation to the Social Services Department about a member of your staff, the senior social worker may call a strategy meeting within 24 hours, which you are required to attend. If the SSD names the member of staff against whom an allegation has been made, that staff member will not be allowed to attend the strategy meeting.

The meeting will be attended by a range of professionals known to the family (if appropriate), including the police. The purpose of the meeting would be to review the facts of the allegation, seek information about the child and the family, find information about the staff member who is alleged to have carried out the abuse, and to decide if there is a case to answer. The Chair may ask if you have suspended the staff member or if you are considering such action. Therefore, given that attendance at a strategy meeting is a distinct possibility, it is advisable that the policy and procedure include very clear information about what could happen at such a meeting and the possible outcomes.

In your policy remember the needs of your staff member. They have a right to receive details of the allegation at the earliest possible opportunity and should be kept informed of the progress of the investigation and of any decisions made.

Write a procedure for an investigation, which might include the following points:

➤ how the timing should be kept short as this will be a stressful time and, if possible, should not be dragged out longer than necessary
➤ who will chair the meeting and who will attend and take the minutes
➤ the issue of confidentiality
➤ the terms and conditions of the meeting
➤ who can make a decision and how the information will be shared and stored
➤ decide what the options are if the allegation is substantiated
➤ include an option to seek legal advice, particularly if termination of employment is considered.

If the allegation is not substantiated, consider what information will be needed on the personal file of the staff member concerned and remember to work in compliance with the Data Protection Act. Finally, agree on how you will inform the original complainant and the child's family. Your child protection policy also needs to include how to resolve a situation where one staff member has informed against another.

NVQ in Management Level 3 links

Element	Knowledge evidence	Personal competencies
A1.2 Maintain healthy, safe and productive working conditions	A1.2 Analytical techniques Communication Health and safety Organisational context Workplace organisation	Building teams Communicating Focusing on results Thinking and taking decisions

Case studies

Below are two case studies that could be used as staff-meeting discussion points. Talk about what you would do and why you would do it. What policies and procedures would you use to support your decision and why?

Over the past few months there have been a number of staff changes in your setting. You make sure that you are keeping within the ratios by using an agency member of staff at present, and you have also recruited a trainee. One of the parents comes to you and complains that her child is having constant accidents in your setting and says that she thinks that this is due to poor supervision since the loss of your staff.

➤ What do you do and why?
➤ What relevant policies and procedures will you use to guide your action?

You manage a setting that is willing to include children with special educational needs. One of the children with special needs continues to demonstrate unprovoked aggressive behaviour, although generally he has made huge improvements. A set of parents come to you complaining about the child, declaring that he is a danger to the other children and demanding that he be removed. They are fearful of his aggressive behaviour and they think that he is a bully. They have started lying in wait for other parents telling them about the child and raising anxieties.

The staff members are very uncertain about what to do because they are pleased that this child is making progress but they are now concerned that he is having a negative impact on the rest of the group. They are also fearful of the parents as their behaviour is increasingly threatening and they have made other parents and carers behave in an equally demanding way.

➤ What do you do and why?
➤ What relevant policies and procedures will you use to guide your action?

Useful information

Key health and safety legislation
Construction (Design and Management) Regulations 1994
Anyone who appoints a designer or contractor has to ensure that they are competent for the work, particularly the person appointed Planning Supervisor and Principal Contractor, and that they will allocate adequate resources for health and safety.

Control of Substances Hazardous to Health Regulations 1999 (COSHH)
They require employers to assess the risks from hazardous substances and take appropriate precautions.

Employers' Liability (Compulsory Insurance) General Regulations 1996

They require employers to take out insurance against accidents and ill health to their employees and display the certificate prominently.

Fire Extinguisher Regulations

Foam, CO_2, dry-powder and halon extinguishers are all red. A colour-coded panel may be fixed on or above the operating instruction panel. The certificate issued by the contractor following the annual maintenance check must be kept available for inspection. Regular visual checks of the equipment must be undertaken and recorded.

Fire Precautions Act 1971

All organisations must make arrangements to assess the risk of fire to both people and property, and steps should be taken to minimise those risks. All properties where more than 20 people are employed at any one time, or where more than ten people are employed at any one time elsewhere than on the ground floor, must have a fire certificate or an exemption certificate issued by the local fire brigade. The certificate must be kept on the premises.

Food Safety Act 1990

Managers have a legal obligation to have food premises and equipment that are designed, maintained and cleaned so that they do not contaminate food. Breaking food laws is a criminal offence. People and companies breaking hygiene law can be fined up to £20,000 or be imprisoned for two years. An individual or company may not be convicted of an offence only if they can prove they have done everything to try to avoid it. In order to achieve this, staff must be trained, management systems must be in place and all records must be kept.

Food Safety (General Food Hygiene) Regulations 1995

These regulations lay down the requirements for premises, including the number of hand basins, protection from pests and so on. They also state that every food business must:

➤ look at the steps involved in storing, preparing, displaying and selling food
➤ identify the potential hazards at each stage
➤ establish the critical control points involved in food safety
➤ control the hazards at each stage and monitor to ensure completion
➤ review the hazard control
➤ keep records such as temperature logs, pest control and so on
➤ check that everything is actually happening at all times.

All these are part of Hazard Analysis and Critical Control Points (HACCP).

Food Safety (Temperature Control) Regulations 1995

These regulations (apart from a few exemptions) state that high-risk foods must either be kept at or below 8°C or above 63°C.

Health and Safety at Work etc Act 1974

Employers who have five or more employees must have a written health and safety policy, communicate it to the staff, have it ready for inspection and review it regularly.

Health and Safety (Display Screen Equipment) Regulations 1992

They set out requirements for employees who use visual display units (VDUs) as a significant part of their work.

Health and Safety (First Aid) Regulations 1981

They cover requirements for first aid.

Health and Safety Information for Employees Regulations 1989

These regulations require employers to display a poster telling employees what they need to know about health and safety.

Health and Safety (Young Persons) Regulations 1997

They require employers to assess and address the risks to young persons, taking into account their immaturity, inexperience and lack of understanding with regards to their health and safety. The regulations define a young person as someone under the age of 18 years.

The risk assessment must also cover the following areas:

➤ workstations and layout
➤ work processes and activities
➤ exposure to harmful agents
➤ use of work equipment
➤ health and safety training.

The assessment must take into account the psychological and physical capabilities of the young person when deciding if they should be barred from certain work.

Management of Health and Safety at Work Regulations 1992 and Management of Health and Safety at Work (Amendment) Regulations 1994

They require employers to carry out risk assessments associated with their work activity which may affect their health and safety. Make arrangements for implementing the health and safety measures identified in the risk assessment, appoint competent people to implement the arrangements, set up emergency procedures and provide clear information and training to all staff (including temporary staff).

Manual Handling Operations Regulations 1992

These require risk assessment of all cases where employees move, lift, push or pull objects by hand or bodily force as part of their employment. Employers need to identify hazards associated with manual handling and ways to reduce risk. They also need to provide employees with advice, information and training. The assessment needs to be reviewed regularly.

Personal Protective Equipment at Work Regulations 1992

Employers are required to provide appropriate protective clothing and equipment for their employees.

Provision and Use of Work Equipment Regulations 1992

These regulations require that the equipment provided for use at work be safe.

Reporting of Injuries, Diseases and Dangerous Occurrences Regulations 1995

These require employers to notify certain occupational injuries, diseases and dangerous occurrences. A revised version came into effect in 1996.

Workplace (Health, Safety and Welfare) Regulations 1992

They cover a wide range of basic health and safety regulations aimed at protecting employees' health from injury or long-term illness, their safety by avoiding immediate danger and their welfare by providing personal comfort at work. This includes ventilation, heating, lighting, clean work environment, workstations, seating, and space, bathroom facilities, drinking water and a safe building within which to work.

Organisations

➤ Back Care, 16 Elmtree Road, Teddington, Middlesex TW11 8ST. Tel: 020-8977 5474. Website: www.backcare.org.uk

➤ Criminal Records Bureau, PO Box 110, Liverpool L3 6ZZ. Information line: 0870-909 0811. Website: www.crb.org.uk

➤ Employer's Forum on Disability, Nutmeg House, 60 Gainsford Street, London SE1 2NY. Tel: 020-7403 3020. Website: www.employers-forum.co.uk

➤ Health and Safety Executive (HSE), HSE Infoline, Caerphilly Business Park, Caerphilly CF83 3GG. Tel: 0870-154 5500. Website: www.hse.org.uk

➤ HSE Books, PO Box 1999, Sudbury, Suffolk CO10 2WA. Tel: 01787-881 165. Website: www.hsebooks.org.uk

➤ Institute of Occupational Safety and Health (IOSH), The Grange, Highfield Drive, Wigston, Leicester LE18 1NN. Tel: 0116-257 3100. Website: www.iosh.co.uk

➤ Mind (The Mental Health Charity), 15–19 Broadway, London E15 4BQ. Tel: 020-8519 2122. Website: www.mind.org.uk

➤ National Society for the Prevention of Cruelty to Children (NSPCC), Weston House, 42 Curtain Road, London EC2A 3NH. Helpline: 0808-800 5000. Website: www.nspcc.org.uk

➤ Royal Society for the Prevention of Accidents, Edgbaston Park, 353 Bristol Road, Birmingham B5 7ST. Tel: 0121-248 2000. Website: www.rospa.co.uk

➤ The Mental Health Foundation, 7th floor, 83 Victoria Street, London SW1H 0HW. Tel: 020-7802 0300. Website: www.mentalhealth.org.uk

Resources

➤ *Health and Safety Law: What You Should Know*, a free leaflet from the Health and Safety Executive that tells you who needs to be trained and how the training can be delivered, and gives advice on the relevant legislation.

➤ *Fire Extinguishers and Safety Equipment* (Wormald Fire Systems), a CD-ROM designed to help organisations fulfil their legal requirements under the Fire Precautions Act 1971. It is a user-friendly interactive CD-ROM endorsed by the Institute of Fire Engineers and the UK Fire Protection Association. Available from Wormald Ansul (UK) Ltd, tel: 0161-205 2321, website: www.water-mist.com

➤ *Misconduct of Teachers and Workers with Children and Young Persons*, a DfEE circular (number 11/95) that includes information about List 99. List 99 contains the names, dates of birth and teacher reference numbers of people whose employment has been barred or restricted, either on grounds of misconduct or on medical grounds.

Chapter 7 Managing finance

- ➤ **Business plan**
- ➤ **Marketing the service**
- ➤ **Managing a budget**
- ➤ **Financial records**
- ➤ **Financial terminology**
- ➤ **Financial procedures**
- ➤ **Fund-raising**

Managers need to understand how to ensure good financial planning and control. This begins with sound strategic business planning, underpinned by clear financial policies and procedures with built-in checking and review processes. Managers must never underestimate the importance of managing the finances well. Without adequate financial controls organisations have no chance of surviving in the longer term. Having a clear understanding of the financial aspects of running a service is therefore critical to its survival.

Business plan

Many small businesses, for example, nurseries, playgroups and after-school clubs, think of strategic business planning as something to be done by large companies. However, the best managed businesses see planning to meet short-, medium- and long-term objectives as key to their successful survival. They use business planning as an opportunity to check:

- ➤ if all their staff know why the business was set up
- ➤ if they know what their shared aims are
- ➤ if they are clear about how they intend to achieve these aims
- ➤ if there are gaps in their service provision
- ➤ if they need to reconsider their purpose
- ➤ if they meet their customers' needs
- ➤ if they are appealing to potential customers
- ➤ what internal and external threats they are facing
- ➤ what action they need to take to survive
- ➤ what they want to improve and develop to meet the challenges.

Writing a business plan is a very useful way of addressing these questions and planning for the year ahead. This is the process where you identify what money is necessary to fund any changes or developments, particularly when considering possible internal and external threats that could have a serious financial impact on the business, for example, spiralling recruitment costs due to high turnover of staff, or increased baby places at the setting to compensate for decreased numbers of older children.

Preparing to write the business plan

Writing the business plan is the last stage of the planning process. The first step is to involve your team and other key people such as governors, trustees and parent representatives. Ask yourself and them, 'Why are we here?' and 'Are we still meeting our original purpose?'. For example, is 'providing teatime clubs to local children' enough or is there a need for breakfast clubs as well? Is 'providing daycare' enough to describe your purpose, or should you be including 'family support' as well? Agree on whether you need to broaden your definition of the setting's mission and objectives. Begin to answer the question, 'Where do we want to be in three to five years?' and consider what the internal and external challenges to the setting are, by doing a **SWOT** analysis with the team. Ask them:

➤ What are the **S**trengths of the service?
➤ What are the **W**eaknesses of the service?
➤ What are the **O**pportunities for the service?
➤ What are the **T**hreats to the service?

Conduct some market research to help you find out if you are still offering the right service or if you need to change some parts of it.

Introduce staff to the concept of financial forecasting so that they understand how planning to develop the service and financial planning are integrated. Explain to them the different sources of finance.

Use this time to review the staff and consider whether you need to reorganise the balance of the team. Do you need more staff to meet your objectives? Is there a skills shortage among staff that must be addressed?

Using this information, agree on your targets for the next year, with some built in over the coming three years. These could be short term, such as making a discovery garden, medium term, such as going through a quality assurance programme, or long term, such as becoming part of the Sure Start programme. It is important to remember that the targets agreed on will need to link to the purpose of your service and will contribute to its development and sustainability.

Finally, build in a performance review so that you know when you have achieved your targets.

Writing the business plan

Use a simple format for the plan, such as:

➤ description of the service and its purpose
➤ management and organisation to achieve the targets
➤ marketing plan (identifying customers' needs)
➤ financial forecast
➤ performance outcomes.

Describe the service

A business plan describes the business, its history and performance to date. For example, you could write, 'Set up in 1989, this school-based breakfast club provides a nutritious breakfast for 24 children aged four to eight years in a safe, comfortable environment, where staff are available to help the children prepare for the school day. Originally offering a service to 16 children, it has expanded to 24 and has a waiting-list of 40 children. It is the first service of its type to achieve the Quality Assurance Award, and last year it received the Local Community Service Award. This year it has been chosen as one of the Lord Mayor's charities'.

Management and organisation
Identify management and organisation, for example, 'Led by a qualified play worker with two years' experience and supported by two unqualified staff and a parent helper. One staff member is currently undertaking her NVQ in Play Work Level 2. If the qualified staff member is absent, the school will ensure that there is a qualified member of staff on site. However, this arrangement is temporary and offered through goodwill'.

Marketing plan
Identify your customers and potential customers through your marketing plan, using information collected from your market research. The marketing plan helps you to ensure that you are targeting the right customer for your service and that there is enough room for you in the market, taking into account all the various competitors (see the section 'Marketing the service' on pages 100 and 101). For example, you could write, 'Our setting provides the only service of its type to children and families predominantly from two local estates, from where the children can walk to the club. The majority of the families work in low-paid jobs so cannot afford large fees for the service'.

Financial forecast
Include a financial forecast demonstrating overall viability. Forecast for at least one year ahead. You need to make enough money to keep the business going, but you also need enough money to pay for bills, staff wages and suppliers. If the business is unlikely to show profitability for a year or two, forecast for three years. Remember to include direct costs, such as breakfast food and overheads, rent, staff wages including national insurance costs, insurance and so on. When producing a financial forecast, include a profit-and-loss forecast, which is the information that gives you an immediate picture of how the business is doing, so that you can remedy emerging gaps and respond to problems. Have a cash-flow forecast as well, so that you can see how much money is coming in and going out on a monthly basis. A business will die if it does not have a regular cash flow. It is a good idea to put in a balance-sheet forecast, so that you can see how you will monitor your forecast against actual progress (see the section 'Financial terminology' section on pages 103 and 104). For example, write, 'Currently the fees pay for the rent of premises and the necessary food costs. However, there is insufficient income to fund any rent increase, to purchase a new cooker or for an additional qualified staff member to reduce the waiting-list of over 40 children and to meet the ratios when the current qualified staff member is absent'.

Performance outcomes
Finally, agree on how and when you will know that you have achieved your targets, and ensure that you share this information with your whole team. Keep the planning process live and have regular review meetings to check progress.

Marketing the service

Marketing is about finding out what your customers want and then satisfying those needs within the organisation's capability. You therefore have to be clear about:

➤ your setting's capability
➤ what you are trying to achieve
➤ who your target market is
➤ how you will promote your organisation.

Market research is the means by which you collect this essential information so as to inform your business development. The more detailed the market research, the more reliable the business planning will be. Use your market research to:

➤ define your position in the market
➤ identify your current and potential customers (as they change, so do their needs and expectations) – try to be as accurate as possible so that you can tailor your business to meet their needs
➤ determine the price that your customer can pay, which is key to financial planning
➤ identify the level of quality that your customers will require (setting your price too low may give the wrong impression if they associate high quality with a particular value)
➤ identify your competitors, what they offer and their strengths and weaknesses. Define who is already out there and if there are gaps in the market.

The marketing campaign

Decide where and how your marketing campaign will take place. Remember that visual impact gives 55 per cent of the impression. Consider the marketing options and decide on the most appropriate, cost-effective methods for you. In early years, word of mouth is a key way of finding out what people want, so you could ask your staff to talk to parents about the service, what they like and what they need. However, you cannot make a judgement on a minority view, so it is important to use more than one marketing method.

Gather information

Use these methods to find out what customers want:

➤ face-to-face interviews with parents
➤ open days or evenings for potential customers
➤ focus groups
➤ questionnaires through a postal survey
➤ using other local research (done by the Early Years Development and Childcare Partnership or through the Children's Information Service)
➤ commissioning some telephone research.

Producing a good questionnaire

Make sure that you get the answers to the right questions:

➤ define your audience
➤ keep the wording simple and jargon-free
➤ be precise – ask questions that give useful answers
➤ ask one question for each answer
➤ put the easy and logical questions first
➤ keep complex matters for the end
➤ ask questions in the past tense
➤ complete a sample trial before conducting the research.

Share information about yourself

Ensure that your potential customers know who you are through:

➤ the local media (develop a good relationship with local journalists, send short stories about your group, considering things from an interesting angle, and so on)
➤ write articles for national specialist magazines
➤ advertise with mail shots and leaflets
➤ look for sponsorship
➤ network
➤ be prepared to do presentations to funding organisations, such as the Learning and Skills Council, EYDCP, Rotary Clubs or local business groups.

Managing a budget

Writing the annual business plan is a long-term activity and the plan may cover two to five years. However, there also needs to be more immediate financial planning, which is done through the allocation of the budget. The budget is a key tool and needs to be managed carefully.

Many businesses run into trouble because they have not planned ahead or do not know how much profit or loss they have made, until it is too late in the year to make any adjustments. However, by using a budget to identify and monitor emerging problems, you are more likely to maintain control over your finances and make the necessary modifications before it is too late.

The budget is agreed within the business plan and it is best to prepare it at least six to twelve months in advance of the beginning of the financial year (April), so that changes and adjustments can be made before it is finalised (ideally a month before the new financial year). Expenditure needs to be categorised, coded and allocated to those with direct operational responsibility. In early years settings, expenditure is often worked out on a 'per child' basis.

Budgets are usually set to control spending, therefore, if you are allocated £350 in the repairs budget, you are expected to balance this budget throughout the year, so that you do not overspend. Sometimes there may be some income-generating targets set within the budget. For example, £15,000 may be allocated for training but the plan has indicated that 10 per cent of that will be generated by taking on

Manager's tip
Consider getting the advice of an accountant but also remember that good book-keeping reduces accountants' time and therefore their costs. You can buy a ready-made system for the computer and, if you are doing payroll, this may be very helpful. It may seem very expensive as an initial outlay, but it could be cost-effective and pay for itself in the long term if it reduces your time and cuts down on your administration.

NVQ candidates. If possible, build in a contingency fund to help you cope with unexpected circumstances; however, you should be careful with this and use it only for emergencies, otherwise it could be used to compensate for poor financial planning.

Managers need to be able to check financial records against the budget on a regular basis. At any time, the records should be able to show how the setting is performing against the budget allocated for the purpose. It would be sensible to analyse the budget progress in detail regularly.

Financial records

All organisations need to keep financial records. They are also required to file accounts on time and to pay legal charges to banks. The records need to show a true and accurate record of the financial activities of an organisation. Managers need to be fully aware of the current financial situation in order to remain in control of what money is coming in and going out. Lack of reliable financial information has been cited as the reason for so many businesses getting into difficulty.

The status of an organisation determines how to keep the records and who has access to them. For example, there are different regulations if your organisation is a charity or a company limited by guarantee. For example, if your setting is a charity and has an expenditure of over £250,000, it must operate within the charity accounting regulations or charity Statement of Recommended Practice (SORP).

The following are groups or people who have access to financial records:

➤ Companies House (Companies Act)
➤ the Charity Commission (a requirement as a registered charity)
➤ any organisation that gives the setting a grant (such as the LEA)
➤ the organisation auditors (their role is to report on whether financial statements have been properly prepared in accordance with company and, where relevant, charity law; a limited company with sales over £350,000 needs to have copies of the audited accounts filed in Companies House)
➤ major funding bodies, such as the National Lottery (website: www.lotterygoodcauses.org.uk/education)
➤ donors (to check that money has been spent on items agreed by them)
➤ trustees, governors and the management committee
➤ the Chief Executive.

Financial records need to be consistent, easy to read, up to date, accurate, and signed and dated by the correct person. If a mistake is made on financial records, it is best to cross out the errors in ink and then rewrite them rather than using white-out liquid.

The following records must be kept:

➤ bank-account records with bank statements filed
➤ fee-collection procedures
➤ fee-arrears procedures (loss of fees can have a detrimental effect on weekly cash flow, the money used to keep salaries and suppliers paid on time)
➤ purchasing-equipment procedures, with details of purchases recorded and dated. It might be easier to have a book for capital expenditure and one for revenue to make it easier when doing your tax returns.

➤ orders from suppliers

➤ records of income

➤ invoice procedures (record of expenditure and invoices and receipts for each entry – all these will be checked by the auditors at the end of the year)

➤ petty-cash procedures

➤ wages and salaries book, including National Insurance records (you may also need an Inland Revenue file for all tax returns and records)

➤ fund-raising (include collection, banking, recording and spending arrangements, as this will be audited).

Manager's tip

It is worth remembering that any financial records could be subject to an audit at any time.

Financial terminology

The balance sheet

You need to be able to see a picture of your business development, and this is what a balance sheet does. It shows you where the money came from and where it was spent, including fixed assets. It should specify all the sources of funding and needs to show your profit and any loans received to date.

Profit and loss account

This is another view of how the business is doing and gives a more immediate picture. The profit and loss information is usually on a monthly basis, although it covers an accounting period of a year. It helps you to identify where there are gaps or problems so that you can take corrective action.

Costs

Some costs are fixed – these include fixed salaries, rent and insurance. They are also called 'overheads'. Other costs are variable and they are usually the direct costs associated with running the service. It is also important not to forget depreciation costs, which are the costs of your assets reducing in value as they are used during the life of your business.

Cash flow

This is like the profit-and-loss account but is more specific in that the picture that it gives shows how money is moving from one source to another. Cash is critical to the business. Many businesses go under because they run into a cash-flow problem, even though their profit potential is very good. You need cash to pay your suppliers, fund your running costs and buy any necessary resources. Planning your cash flow therefore means thinking about how much leeway you can give people about paying fees. You also need to negotiate some credit with suppliers to give you time to pay bills, but remember to take account of depreciation in your costs and other payments such as the VAT, which will be a cash settlement.

Assets

An asset is the capital wealth of a business. It is the real physical resources and is used by businesses to create a permanent basis of wealth. Assets usually have a life of more than a year. Fixed assets are usually land, buildings, equipment, computers, fixtures and fittings.

Current assets are short term and will turn into cash in the next year. The importance of current assets is that they show how much an organisation has in the way of cash or near-cash, and that, in turn, tells you how viable the business is. There are three main types of current assets:

➤ stock
➤ debtors (people who have bought goods or service and owe money)
➤ other monies (includes petty cash, short-term deposits and other monies owed).

Current assets in a business should be 'liquid' (as close to cash as possible). Limited companies must keep a capital register, including all the capital items that they own. This also records the disposal of any of these items and the cumulative depreciation.

Liabilities

A liability is a debt payable outside the business which will have to be met in the future. Typical liabilities are long term and should become short term and paid off. These would include money owed for goods purchased, bank overdrafts, short-term debt and taxation due, dividends such as monies payable to shareholders, sums owed to leasing companies and accruals, otherwise known as monies put away for something that has happened but for which, as yet, there is no proof of payment.

Reserves

There are two types of reserves. Firstly profit which is cash and is ploughed back into the business is called a 'revenue reserve'. This can be used to buy stock or assets. The other type of reserve is 'capital reserve'. This is paper-based profit, for example, where the value of the nursery building has increased because of local property price rises, so that on paper the business is worth more. This money can be used as collateral for a loan but cannot be translated into cash.

Financial procedures

Consider having procedures about the management of:

➤ petty cash (who signs and how much do you spend on what)
➤ banking (how often and who goes)
➤ fund-raising, such as rules about raffle tickets
➤ purchasing or procurement. For example, get at least two quotes before purchasing a large item or engaging building, repairs and maintenance services. Look for good value rather than cheap prices and always try to negotiate a discount. Consider whether it is better to lease rather than buy, for example, equipment such as photocopiers. Check if you can purchase in bulk through local groups. Do you ask willing volunteers, such as parents, for help to repair, replace or purchase equipment? Do you use an approved list of reliable suppliers rather than rely on the standard catalogues?

Fees policy

It is very important that fees be paid on time because late fees will cost you both directly and indirectly. You need to show parents that you are serious about your fees policy, because people soon get to know if you are prepared to act on what you say. Have a system to discourage late fees and a procedure for chasing them, for example, penalty payments, a reminder letter from the manager or senior member of the organisation, or a threat of Small Claims Court.

You may have a system to help parents who get into real difficulty, such as a reduced-fee system. However, if you do this you need a set of criteria that is applied fairly and consistently, and there should be no barriers to information.

You also need a system to ensure that parents do not take their children from the group without giving notice, so that they pay for their last month's service. You may charge one month's fees as a non-refundable deposit as insurance that parents will not leave with four weeks' fees outstanding. The issue of notice payment has become more of a problem because of the number of children being offered school places at short notice. There are arguments for and against registration fees. These may reduce the number of parents putting their children's names on every list, but they may also prove a real barrier to applying for a much-needed place.

Taking and recording fees

When taking fees from parents and carers either by cash or cheque, it is important to issue a receipt because it is the only proof of payment and registration that you have. Receipts should be in duplicate: the top copy for the parent and the bottom copy for the setting record. Receipts should be individually numbered, contain the amount, date, child's name and the period that the fee covers, and should be signed by an authorised member of staff.

Fees should be recorded in the nursery attendance register, showing the amount collected and the receipt number, as the registers and the fee receipt books are inspected as part of the annual audit.

Using the Small Claims Court

This court is to help people resolve disputes involving a small amount of money (under £5000). Sometimes, using the Small Claims Court may cost as much as the debt or more if you fail to resolve the dispute, but it is quite a useful financial strategy. You can make a claim by getting an application form from the County Court.

Fund-raising

Fund-raising in the traditional sense conjures up a picture of a parent committee running a fun day, or the staff organising a Christmas bazaar, summer picnic, firework party, auction, bring-and-buy sale or barn dance. These are good ways to raise money for building repairs, specific equipment or a trip out. However, fund-raising needs to be considered within a wider context. For many settings in the voluntary and charitable sectors, fund-raising is an essential part of the annual budget. Some organisations employ a fund-raising manager to lead this task. They will investigate grant-making trusts, government funding, payroll giving, donations, bequests and sponsorships to gain capital and revenue funding. In smaller settings staff may write to local businesses asking for free gifts to raffle at parents' evenings or at the Christmas play.

Finding free services also fits under the remit of fund-raising. For example, big companies often have a community-support initiative where they identify some local charities and services that help them through challenges. This may include landscaping the garden, painting a mural, redecorating an area of the setting, and making or refurbishing a piece of equipment. There are also companies that donate free paper, paint, fabrics and other materials that could furnish the creative cupboard for some time.

The business plan and the fund-raising targets need to be linked closely together. Targets set in the business plan, such as improving musical resources, could be part of the annual fund-raising challenges. Getting money for capital bids is usually easier than revenue funding. People are happy to be

Manager's handbook **early years training & management**

associated with a new sensory room but less keen to fund the cleaning materials for a year. However, involving parents, carers and supporters in fund-raising activities can have a very powerful motivating response, even if little money is raised. Sharing the challenge for the benefit of the children can bring out the best in people and encourage communication among those who would not usually talk to each other.

Funds can also be raised through financial lenders or investors. These companies will need guarantees that you can repay the money. If you borrow from the bank they will charge an interest rate and want to see steady growth in your business if they are to continue lending you money.

Risk capital, which is often associated with fast-growing businesses, is usually given by venture capitalists. They will be looking for winners so, as a manager, you need a good business plan and effective negotiation skills if you are to successfully achieve funding from such places. The cost of this kind of investment is usually a management fee paid up front or annually. Bear in mind that the venture company may also put a member of their board on your management board to look after its interests.

Grants available through Government funding

Most of the Government money comes through the childcare grant allocated to each Local Education Authority and Early Years Development and Childcare Partnership (EYDCP) on the basis of the numbers of children aged between one year and fourteen years in the area, with further adjustments for levels of deprivation.

The EYDCPs have also been given funds to employ business support staff to develop and improve the business and financial competence of childcarers. There is money available for childcare services for children with special needs, towards training childcare workers and childminder support.

There are a large number of organisations that administer grants for early years settings (see the *A–Z of Finding Funds Directory of Funding for Early Years* in the section 'Useful information' on page 108).

NVQ in Management Level 3 links

Elements	Knowledge evidence	Personal competencies
B1.1 Make recommendations for the use of resources *B1.2* Contribute to the control of resources	*B1.1* and *B1.2* Analytical techniques Communication Involvement and motivation Organisational context Resource management	Communicating Focusing on results Thinking and taking decisions

Case study

Below is a case study that could be used as a staff-meeting discussion point. Talk about what you would do and why you would do it. What policies and procedures would you use to support your decision and why?

You manage a small playgroup where a large number of the children are aged three years plus and attend on a sessional basis. Up to now the playgroup has been well supported but on your return from the Christmas break you lose five full-time children to local schools, with no notice. One of the head teachers tells you that they are expanding their Reception class to take more three-year-olds in order to benefit from the Government funding. What do you do? Why? What relevant policies and procedures will you use to guide your action?

Things to consider:

➤ writing a business plan
➤ where to seek funds
➤ writing funding applications
➤ ideas for fund-raising.

Useful information

➤ *A–Z of Finding Funds Directory of Funding for Early Years* (Department for Education and Skills). Tel: 0845-602 2260 (DfES publications helpline).

➤ The Charity Commission, Harmsworth House, 13–15 Bouverie Street, London EC4Y 8DP. Tel: 0870-333 0123. Website: www.charity-commission.gov.uk

➤ National Council for Voluntary Childcare Organisations (NCVCCO), Unit 4, Pride Court, 80–82 White Lion Street, London N1 9PF. Tel: 020-7833 3319. Website: www.ncvcco.org.uk

➤ The Chartered Institute of Management Accountants (CIMA), 26 Chapter Street, London SW1P 4NP. Tel: 020-7663 5441. Website: www.cima.org.uk

➤ Inland Revenue, tel: 020-7667 4001 (enquiry line) or 0845-607 0143 (New Employers helpline). Website: www.inlandrevenue.gov.uk

➤ AccountingWEB, website: www.accountingweb.co.uk

➤ Enterprise Advisory Service International, website: www.govgrants.com This site provides up-to-date information and advice on business grants to help companies identify the financial and practical help that they need.

Chapter 8 Managing meetings

> ➤ **Managing the meeting**
> ➤ **Participating in meetings**
> ➤ **Different types of meetings**
> ➤ **Writing the minutes**

Meetings are a tried and tested way for people to pass on information, solve problems, discuss issues, brainstorm ideas and motivate and sell themselves. No matter what kind of meeting you attend, you need to be aware of the impact that you have at all times, whether it is by your participation in the meeting or lack of it.

Meetings can be used in many ways – your attitude to each will determine how well you use it and how other people see you. Meetings are best used as learning and development opportunities, where those attending them leave motivated, informed and clear about their responsibilities. In order to ensure that meetings are well used, managers need to know how to chair them and minute them, what makes them successful and to encourage participation. As a manager, you will need to attend many meetings, so use them well and make them work for you.

Managing the meeting

A well-run meeting can be a very engaging and invigorating experience. The effective management of meetings can make a huge difference to the functioning of your setting, and the chairperson will be appreciated for making things happen.

The role of the chairperson

The position of the person who chairs a meeting is an interesting one. He or she is responsible for ensuring that it is properly conducted, kept in order and that the business of the meeting is addressed. The chairperson is in a key position of authority and must not abuse this position. A good chairperson will:

➤ run an efficient and well-balanced meeting – this means that they get through more business, avoid time-wasting and give greater opportunity for participation

and discussion
➤ be prepared, have read the minutes in advance and know the facts about the points on the agenda
➤ get there early to network and iron out any particular difficulties before the meeting begins
➤ need to be calm and friendly, especially as he or she sets the tone of the meeting
➤ have a sound knowledge of procedure – this is important because there are often different rules for different meetings
➤ bring a sense of humour to the meeting to help create a balanced atmosphere (a witty comment used sensitively can often be the most effective way of defusing bad humour or conflict in the meeting)

➤ focus on the big issues and avoid getting caught up in the minutiae of the debate

➤ be able to think clearly and objectively: their summation of a situation is very important because it has to be fair and balanced and reflect all the varying viewpoints put forward in the meeting, so that everyone agrees on the action point

➤ always keep complete control of his or her temper and never resort to sarcasm and impatience

➤ speak clearly and loudly so that everyone can hear him or her

➤ insist that all comments and questions be made through him or her (some people like to be addressed as Madam Chair or Mr Chairman, so make it clear to the members of the meeting how you want to be addressed)

➤ ensure that everyone is seen and heard at the meeting, for example, by requesting that they stand when they speak

➤ start and finish a meeting on time and state when the meeting has finished by saying, for example, 'Well, that concludes the meeting, thank you everyone'.

By virtue of the office, the chairperson takes precedence over all other people who are present at the meeting that he or she is presiding. His or her ruling on any matter of procedure is final.

If a meeting loses confidence in the chairperson, the members can eject him or her by moving a motion, for example, 'That this meeting has no confidence in the chairperson'. This has to be seconded and put to the meeting. If the resolution is carried by the majority, the person must vacate the role of chairperson. The meeting can then either continue with the business or elect another person to act as chair. This is rather unusual but useful to know as a means of dealing with unfair or incompetent chairpeople. This situation would usually cause the resignation of the chairperson as it implies no confidence in their general abilities.

The chairperson usually has a casting vote that they can use when there is an equal number of votes for and against the resolution. If the chairperson is nominating themselves for re-election, they cannot preside during the actual period when the election is taking place. If they are re-elected at the meeting, for example, the annual general meeting (AGM), they can return to the chair once the election is complete.

Before the meeting

You will need an agenda for a meeting, so this will need to be drawn up in advance. There may be a system where people are contacted by telephone or e-mail before the meeting and asked if there are any items that they want to add to the agenda. Alternatively, you may put the agenda on a notice-board and invite your staff to add items. Whatever your system, the chairperson will decide which items will be discussed.

Items for discussion have to link to the purpose of the meeting. For example, if you are chairing a subgroup of the Early Years Development and Childcare Partnership with a lead officer to support you, always agree on the agenda together so that you are both prepared and have the correct information for the meeting. Having a subject suddenly sprung on you could be highly embarrassing.

Use the agenda to help you structure the meeting. For example, you may have regular slots for key issues, for example, health and safety or special needs, so that such issues remain in the forefront of the staff members' minds. If there has been a recent change in practice in your setting, it is probably a good idea to have that on the agenda until everyone is familiar with it.

The agenda
The agenda should include:

Welcome

Apologies for absence

Minutes of the last meeting
If these minutes have been circulated, they do not need to be read aloud, although sometimes it is helpful to ask, 'Any changes to page 1, page 2...?' and then to check that everyone agrees that they are a correct record of the last meeting. The chairperson then signs the main copy. If there are any inaccuracies, he or she can make amendments in ink and initial the changes. When the minutes are corrected and agreed, the chairperson of the present meeting signs them. This person does not need to have been at the previous meeting, because he or she is signing on behalf of the members who were there.

The signed copies should be kept in a folder clearly marked 'Minutes book'. They are a permanent and legal record and should be treated in the same way as other legal documents.

Matters arising from the minutes
This is to check progress of the action agreed at the last meeting. By going through matters arising, full discussion can ensue about ongoing issues. It is sensible to have these on the agenda, otherwise the meeting becomes badly timed and other items may be squeezed out. Knowing what may come up through matters arising is vital for the chairperson – they will need to have planned a response.

Review of the action points
Check the progress for action. If the action points were not achieved, reset new action points with new time targets.

Items for discussion

Any other business
This section can be a trap for an unwary chairperson. Any other business (AOB) should be for minor items that have not been included on the agenda. Sometimes people try to use this section to rush through measures without adequate discussion, working on the premise that by the end of the meeting people have started to switch off or prepare to leave. No major matter should be put to the vote under AOB.

Date and time of the next meeting

Starting the meeting

Ensure that the following procedures are put into practice:

➤ You may need to chase people up before the meeting, so it is always worth having a reminder on the meeting agenda to read the minutes before coming to the meeting and for people to bring their copy of the minutes with them.
➤ Start promptly and on time; avoid waiting for latecomers to arrive.
➤ Remind everyone of the purpose of the meeting. Be absolutely clear about it and keep it in mind all through so that you can bring people back to the main task.
➤ If it helps, put the main purpose of the meeting on a card in front of you and use that to keep the meeting in order.
➤ Check why everyone present is attending: is it to give information, or to explain things? If people are attending only to get information from the meeting, consider whether it would be better if they simply had the minutes.
➤ If you are the chairperson of a committee, you must understand the purpose of the committee and the purpose of the meeting.
➤ Try to keep the number of people attending the meeting low to allow for discussion and completion of the task. If somebody cannot come, you may agree on a replacement if this will benefit the meeting.
➤ Appoint someone to take the minutes and to share in some of the work of the meeting.

Throughout the meeting

The chairperson must keep control of the meeting, which means maintaining a brisk pace. They must ensure that everyone has time to make their contributions and they must know when to say, 'Thank you for your contribution, but perhaps you could make the final arrangements after the meeting'.

The chairperson should always remain polite but, at the same time, be able to interrupt in order to keep the speaker to the point. Using humour here can help reduce the chances of offending! If someone is speaking for too long, the chairperson might interject and say, 'Would you like to sum up your main points, please?'.

As well as having to stop people from talking too much during the meeting and monopolising it, the chairperson needs to try to draw contributions from

those who are quiet or who have not spoken. Many people find formal meetings very daunting and may be too anxious, inexperienced or overwhelmed to say anything. The chairperson must remember them and give them the opportunity to contribute, without making them feel that they are being put on the spot.

The chairperson needs to be able to call the meeting to order when she feels that the agenda items have been fully discussed. She then needs to summarise the general discussion. It is sometimes useful to ask everyone to summarise their view of the debate in one sentence. By using this method, the chairperson will find that people learn to be concise. If she does this regularly at meetings, they will get used to her style and learn the art of a succinct sentence.

The chairperson will then tie up the discussion with recommendations and decisions for action, for example, by saying, 'I confirm that we all agree that Sarah will develop an evaluation form and circulate it for comments by 21 February'.

Immediately after the meeting, the chairperson should agree on the minutes with the minute-taker and ensure that they are produced and distributed promptly.

Participating in meetings

Before attending a meeting, consider your attitude to it. Do you feel that the meeting is a waste of time but you have to attend, or do you enjoy meetings and find that you always learn something? Your attitude to the meeting will play a big part in how well you use it and in the impression that you will give to other people at the meeting.

Read the minutes in advance and check that you have completed any action with your name against it. Prepare for the meeting by reading the agenda and any papers that have been distributed.

It has been found that at the start of a meeting, participants' impressions of you are largely neutral if they have never met you before; however, they will soon turn negative if you do not speak up or ask questions. Therefore, you should contribute to the meeting early and ask timely and relevant questions.

It is sensible to adopt certain behaviour when attending a meeting. Address comments through the chairperson and, if you are the chairperson yourself, ensure that all comments are addressed through you to avoid the meeting becoming noisy and uncontrolled. Help the chairperson to keep order by not joining sideline conversations.

Learn to link your comments and follow them through, for example, 'I agree with Sunita, it is a good move' or 'I feel that Roger's earlier point is relevant here and shows us that...'.

Get to the point and do not waffle. Remember that people get bored and lose interest quickly as attention spans are short. Keep your comments sharp and relevant.

Tips for successful meetings

➤ Prepare properly – this is the key to making a positive impact.

➤ Read the minutes of the last meeting and any papers circulated in advance. That way you can contribute, offer your thoughts and ask pertinent questions.

Presenting information at a meeting

➤ If you are speaking to an agenda item, remember that the purpose of presenting information is to:
  ● inform
  ● sell or persuade

- stimulate thought and discussion
- entertain
- promote your setting
- promote yourself.

➤ Consider why you are communicating the information and reflect this in your presentation. Do not say too much, because you will flood your audience with details that will actually detract from the main message. Never speak for more than 20 minutes, and if it has to be longer, split the session by introducing questions. When you try to share information with people that are not part of your group, avoid jargon and talk in plain English. This does not devalue the presentation, it just makes it clearer.

➤ Allow your pace to vary from fast to something more measured. Let your passion and enthusiasm dictate it, but when you want to reinforce certain points be more measured.

➤ Break up your information. Use inflection to highlight emphasis and importance. Think about where you will put the emphasis in a sentence.

➤ Build in pauses to let the message sink in.

➤ Check out your audience to get a response, even if it is only a grunt!

➤ Keep eye contact, as a checking mechanism, especially if you are relying on written cards to help you. When you have read a sentence, look up, make eye contact and then move on.

➤ Avoid filling the silence gaps, otherwise you will end up talking too much.

➤ Anticipate the questions that you may be asked and prepare some answers. Consider the most difficult questions, especially if you are presenting possible change. If the questions are hostile, keep your replies calm and polite.

➤ If you do not know the answer, be honest and say so. Ask for the advice of the audience or refer them to another source of information.

Main problems in meetings

➤ Most meetings do not stick to rules of timeliness or keeping to the point.

➤ People do not address the meeting through the chairperson and the meeting becomes disordered and noisy.

➤ People do not read the minutes of the last meeting before the next meeting.

➤ Meetings are seen as a talking shop where nothing gets done. People often talk too much because they:

- are keen to demonstrate how much they know about a subject
- want to be helpful
- want to demonstrate that they have done their homework
- just love their subject
- are allowed to waffle on as the chairperson does not intervene to call them to order.

➤ People bring quite complex items under 'Any other business'.

➤ The chairpeople and managers do not regularly evaluate the effectiveness of the meeting.

Different types of meetings

Staff meetings

The staff meeting is a very useful meeting for team bonding, sharing information, considering group issues, addressing staff concerns and ensuring that information is understood and implemented. Staff meetings need to follow the guide for any meeting and be well prepared, with every staff member understanding the significance of the meeting.

The manager may not always chair the meeting. By rotating the roles of chairperson and minute-taker, you will provide a good development opportunity for staff members. However, you can put items on the agenda which have training and development purposes. Using a video, brainstorming or case studies to raise awareness about an area of practice all help staff to get a personal insight into their own knowledge or gaps. This also gives you useful information about areas of learning for staff and yourself.

Staff meetings are good opportunities to motivate the team. It is a good idea to provide nice biscuits, cakes or savouries and beverages reflecting the taste of your staff. This shows that you value their coming together and appreciate their efforts. The staff meeting, when well managed, is a good way of bringing the staff member together to learn from each other and to develop as a team.

A staff meeting is also very useful to influence attitudes by way of information and experience, as staff can share these in the meeting.

You may want to consider whether brainstorming is a good, appropriate process for these meetings. Brainstorming is a means of getting people to offer spontaneous ideas to generate new thoughts and approaches or respond to a problem posed. Advertising executive Alex Osborne from the United States of America developed the technique in the 1950s after concluding that typical decision-making processes inhibit rather than encourage creativity.

Brainstorming was considered a positive means of getting the ideas flowing; the practical and operational aspects could be worked on later. The usual mode of brainstorming was that the group should not comprise more than eight people, all suggestions were welcomed, the more bizarre the better, and criticism discouraged. It was positively received because it encouraged open sharing of ideas (it was not just the boss who had ideas) and it was quite a motivating way of involving people.

However, the problem is that at the end of a brainstorming session you have a list of ideas, no plan or solutions, and the original issue may still remain. This lack of conclusion and order caused staff to become dissatisfied because they could not see how they could move forward. Research by Camacho and Paulus (1995)

proved that people produce more ideas working alone than in groups. Camacho and Paulus also found that anxious people did less well in groups. Therefore, for effective brainstorming, they suggest that if time is short and you are under pressure, use individuals working alone to generate ideas, but when you want the ideas to be accepted, involve the group.

To make best use of brainstorming in a group, give people the opportunity to brainstorm alone first and then bring their ideas along to the meeting. There the group can work on the plan or solution together.

Public meetings

You may be called on to organise a public meeting. There are certain procedures appropriate to that meeting. You are likely to have an invited speaker and your role will be to manage the meeting. The usual format is:

Opening remarks

These include welcoming the audience and mentioning the work of your organisation. Link in the subject that the speaker will talk about if appropriate, then introduce the speaker. Do not assume that other people all know who he or she is; give a full introduction, though avoid gushing! Refer to the question-and-answer session that will follow the speech, then call on the speaker to begin.

Questions and answers

When the speaker has finished, call for questions, for example, by saying, 'I would like to invite the audience to ask questions in response to such a stimulating speech!'. When somebody in the audience raises their hand, invite them to stand and state their name before asking their question. Keep them to the point and move them on where necessary, then, when the speaker has answered, say, 'Thank you, and now I would like to take a few more questions...'. Remember that people attending the meeting may be shy or anxious about asking a question, so you ought to have one ready to start the question-and-answer session.

Summary

After the questions, you should make a brief summary, for example, 'Thank you for your questions, I am sure that the whole debate has sparked off some interesting ideas to ponder on'.

Thanks

Propose the vote of thanks, for example, 'I would like to ask Eleanor Gates to thank our speaker'. Then close the meeting, usually ending with thanking all those who have helped to organise it.

Annual general meetings (AGMs)

Format

The usual format is:

➤ apologises for absence
➤ minutes of the last AGM

➤ chairperson's address (brief overview of the work of the organisation over the past year)

➤ annual report from the secretary (reads report)

➤ annual report from the treasurer (reads report)

➤ adoption of the reports (for example, moved by Mrs Franconi and seconded by Mr Miller). When the reports have been read, the chairperson will call on a member of the organisation to adopt the reports and on another member to second the motion. They must be members of the organisation to do this.

➤ election of officers and executive committee. If the chairperson is up for re-election, he or she also stands down at this point and someone else continues the meeting until he or another person is elected.

➤ to consider recommendations that... (this is to get the approval of the meeting for any matters that have already been agreed and worked out by the executive committee)

➤ any other business.

Unlike usual meetings, if a major subject comes up under 'Any other business', it has to be thrashed out and, if necessary, a decision must be made. It may also be decided that the subject will have to be taken forward to future executive meetings for fuller discussion.

Annual report

The annual report is produced for the annual general meeting. This report is critical in that it gives supporters and funders of the organisation an overview of the past year.

The annual report should be interesting and well presented, and the financial report should offer information in a clear and comprehensible format, including graphs and diagrams rather than lots of figures.

Some key meeting terms

Motion	A subject proposed for discussion at the meeting. It is sometimes called a proposal.
Resolution	The same motion after it has been voted upon and agreed.
Amendment	Alters the wording of the motion without changing the intention.
Points of order	These are called when there is an incorrect procedure or when the speaker at the meeting has gone off the subject, is using offensive language or is making insulting insinuations.

Writing the minutes

Minutes are a record of what has happened at a meeting. It is a legal record of the organisation's business.

Minutes are for people who in the future need, or want, to know what the group has discussed or agreed. These may be people who were not at the meeting, or those who were but need to be reminded of what happened.

Minutes are used to find out:

➤ what was decided
➤ why it was decided
➤ what else was reported or discussed
➤ what action the reader is supposed to take and when
➤ what action others are supposed to take and when.

A minute-taker must record information, the main points of the discussion and any decisions accurately and clearly, and in such a way that everything can be easily located and understood in future.

Allocate this task to one person or have a rota so that everyone learns how to do it. Make sure that they know how to take relevant notes. Discourage others from taking too many notes as there is no point in duplication and staff rarely hear what is being said if they are concentrating on writing.

Key information on the minutes

➤ name of the organisation
➤ title of the meeting (for example, 'Staff meeting', 'Management meeting' or 'Health and safety meeting')
➤ date (including the year) and time of the meeting
➤ place of the meeting
➤ members present
➤ other people present and in what capacity (for example, as visitors or guest speakers)
➤ names of the chairperson and minute-taker
➤ apologies for absence
➤ corrections, if any, to the minutes of the previous meeting and proof that the minutes were accepted as an accurate record and signed
  ➤ matters arising from the previous minutes, not covered elsewhere
  ➤ a separate minute for each item or topic covered at the meeting
  ➤ date, time and place of the next meeting, and who will chair and minute this if different.

Taking effective minutes

➤ Use the same headings as those that are on the agenda, to identify every item easily.
➤ Single out each minute clearly with a brief heading that is underlined, in bold or in capital letters.
➤ Clearly separate items with a blank line.
➤ Follow your organisation's format for taking minutes – this will guide the amount to include (depending on whether you have individual minute

sheets, template forms or a minute book), under headings such as 'Topic', 'Main points', 'Decision', 'Who' and 'When', all filled during the meeting.

➤ Decide on how much to include in the minutes by asking yourself, 'If I wasn't at this meeting, what would I need to know?' or 'Could I tell what happened from the meeting minutes?'.

➤ Make sure that you record decisions, major factors leading to decisions and what needs to be done.

➤ Refer to any attachments that have been circulated with the agenda, or that will be circulated with the minutes, and briefly summarise them in the minutes. Make sure that everyone, including people who were not at the meeting, receives the attachments.

➤ Keep the minutes impartial and factual and do not include judgemental words or remarks on people's emotions.

➤ Ask the chairperson to summarise what has been said if you are unclear about what has been decided, or read out your notes and ask the meeting to confirm that they are accurate.

➤ Keep your notes legible so that you can interpret them correctly.

➤ Use headings and subheadings when taking notes during the meeting to keep items separate.

➤ Leave a few lines between each item to make it easier to add further points if they come up later in the meeting. One idea when taking notes is to use a column on the left-hand side of the sheet to star particularly important points and to indicate the initials or name of the person who made each point.

➤ Write up the minutes as soon as possible after the meeting.

➤ Keep your notes until the minutes have been approved at the next meeting, in case there are any queries.

➤ Agree on the minutes with the chairperson and circulate them as quickly as possible. This helps people who were not at the meeting to keep up to date with what is happening, and reminds people of what needs doing. Any documents that were distributed at the meeting should be sent to people who were not there.

➤ Check the confidentiality of items with the chairperson and confirm what you should do. In some cases the chairperson will keep notes of confidential items, in other cases the minute-taker will be asked to minute the item but give the final version to the chairperson or someone else rather than including it in the circulated minutes. Even if an item is confidential, notes or minutes should always be taken. After the meeting they should be kept in an appropriate place. The chairperson needs to indicate where they should be kept and who should have access to them. The chairperson must also ensure that everyone at the meeting is aware that the item is confidential and what this means.

Manager's tip

Use the photocopiable sheet 'Self-assessment of performance at meetings' on page 170 to evaluate how useful your meetings are.

NVQ in Management Level 3 links

Element	Knowledge evidence	Personal competencies
D1.3 Hold meetings	*D1.3* Communication Leadership styles Meetings Organisational context	Acting assertively Building teams Communicating Influencing others Searching for information Thinking and taking decisions

Case studies

Below are two case studies that could be used as staff-meeting discussion points. Talk about what you would do and why you would do it.

You have a staff meeting every six weeks. There is usually a very long agenda and much of the items are minor operational points that often lead to long-winded and unproductive arguments. In addition, the team is diverse and some members are very forceful and will talk at length, while others are very quiet. Recently, you noticed two staff members raising their eyes upwards every time you spoke.

What do you need to do to make the meetings more productive, help all staff to participate and ensure that all key issues are addressed?

You are the chairperson of the local childminding association and you will be organising the first annual general meeting soon. You are nervous about doing this. Devise an action plan, identifying all the tasks necessary to organise an effective meeting, including a list of the related tasks, for example:

➤ who to invite
➤ what information will need to be available
➤ how the meeting will be structured.

Chapter 9 Preparing for inspection

> ➤ **Who inspects?**
> ➤ **The inspection format**
> ➤ **The inspection information**
> ➤ **Preparing for the inspection**
> ➤ **The inspection visit**
> ➤ **The inspection outcome**
> ➤ **If you do not agree with the judgement**
> ➤ **The post-inspection plan**
> ➤ **School inspections**

For many early years staff, the prospect of an inspection brings fear and trepidation. They become worried about being observed and questioned and, for some, it can feel like an examination. However, you, as manager, can turn the inspection around and encourage your staff to see it as a means of celebrating what you do well. Take control and prepare well, so that you are all channelling your energy positively.

The inspector is coming to see how you comply with the National Standards. He or she is looking for you to show that you understand what is expected of you and your staff, and what you do every day to meet the requirements of the National Standards. Take control of the process, prepare properly, understand what is expected of you and be involved in the inspection. An effective inspection is a reciprocal means of sharing your views, explaining your rationale and coming to an agreement about what needs to happen through informed discussion.

Who inspects?

Under the structure for the regulation of inspections, OFSTED's Early Years Directorate regulates and inspects all childminding and daycare services for children under eight years. OFSTED is also responsible for issuing guidance on how to meet the National Standards. Local Education Authorities (LEAs) remain responsible for securing the provision of support services for day nurseries, including providing information, advice and training. In many boroughs and counties, the Early Years Development and Childcare Partnerships (EYDCPs) play an important part in co-ordinating the retained information, advice and training functions.

The inspection format

Every early years setting that used to be inspected under Section 10 of the Children Act 1989 will now be inspected against the 14 National Standards.

According to the introduction to the Standards, they represent a baseline of quality below which no provider must fall. They are also written to give providers a clear message about the principle of continuous improvement.

Each of the 14 Standards describes a quality outcome and is accompanied by a set of supporting criteria that helps you understand what is expected and how you can show that the Standard has been met. The criteria have been written to take account of the following types of daycare: full daycare, sessional daycare, crèches, out-of-school care and childminders. There also annexes, for example, on overnight care and baby care, which tell you what is needed if you provide such a service.

The inspection is outcome-based, which means that you have to show the inspector how you meet each of the Standards. If the inspector identifies weaknesses in the provision, you will have to demonstrate how you will deal with the issue. The emphasis is on you engaging with the inspector to come to a shared agreement, rather than the inspector telling you what to do.

If you operate two different services on one premise, for example, daycare and after-school club, the inspector will try to combine the inspection for the same day. One report will be produced but any conditions or actions will be separate for each service. It is likely that you will have just one inspector, although you may get a new inspector accompanying a more experienced one. Some larger services may have two inspectors.

The inspection information

In advance you will receive a letter giving you a period of time within which your inspection will take place. This is usually within a month. Attached to the letter is a diary sheet where you can tell the inspector which dates you will not be available. In addition, there will be an update form, which you must complete as it gives the inspector the most up-to-date information about the service that you offer. This form covers the following information:

➤ description of the setting
➤ manager's details
➤ details of the organisation and, where appropriate, charity number or company registration number
➤ names and titles of committee members, director of the governing body, identifying chairperson, treasurer and secretary
➤ nominated person's details
➤ premises' details
➤ details of provision (age of children, number of children on the register, information regarding Government funding)
➤ list of people on the premises looking after children and other people working or living on the premises.

Note that the 'registered person' is the individual or corporate body, such as the company, association or committee. He or she has overall responsibility for the provision and is legally responsible for ensuring compliance with the National Standards regulations and any conditions imposed by OFSTED. Where the registered person is a company, society or organisation, he or she asked to nominate a person to act as a contact point with OFSTED.

The 'nominated person' is the person who, for administrative reasons, represents the registered person where this is a company, organisation or society. The registered person still remains the person who is legally responsible.

The 'person in charge' is the person who has day-to-day responsibility for the provision of daycare. This is usually the manager or supervisor.

Ask some or all parents to complete the OFSTED questionnaire. They can either return it to the setting or send it straight to OFSTED. It asks the questions:

➤ Are you happy with the service?
➤ Is there anything that you particularly like?
➤ Is there anything that could be improved?
➤ Are you happy with the information that you receive about your child's care and learning?
➤ Could it be improved?
➤ If you were unhappy with the care, would you know where and how to make a complaint?

Preparing for the inspection

Before the inspection takes place, be fully prepared:

➤ Read the Care Standards Act 2000 and the Guidelines.
➤ Give copies of the Standards to all staff and ask them to read them, paying particular attention to the areas for which they have special responsibility, such as health and safety, child protection or personal and social development.
➤ Read the *Special Educational Needs Code of Practice* and check that your setting's special needs policy and procedures meet the necessary requirements of the Code.
➤ Read the QCA/DfEE document *Curriculum Guidance for the Foundation Stage*.
➤ Arrange a staff meeting to go through the Standards and check that all the staff understand what each one means.
➤ Read the last inspection report and check that all recommendations and requirements have been met.
➤ Allocate lead staff an area to consider. For example, give the SENCO National Standards 9, 10 and 11 and ask them to check that you can show how you meet the Standards. Make sure that they audit the areas so that they can see if there are gaps in the resources.
➤ Devise a quiz to check learning and remind everyone how they meet the Standards every day.
➤ Start collecting evidence of how you meet the Standards. Use the photocopiable sheets 'OFSTED inspection preparation plan' on pages 171–173 to help you do this.
➤ Allocate members of staff an Early Learning Goal each and ask them to put a book together of photographs and samples of the children's work which shows how you are helping children to meet the Goals. Place these books in the book corner for the children, or use them to show new and potential parents the kind of activities and experiences that you offer.
➤ Look at the displays and make any necessary improvements.
➤ Collect evidence of staff training and development.

➤ Put a check-list on the notice-board and invite your staff to add what they consider to be evidence showing how you meet the Standards.
➤ Tell parents about the impending inspection and what to expect.

Improving your provision
Use the whole process as a way of reviewing your practice and improving the service that you deliver. Think about:

➤ the quality of relationships with the children, staff and parents
➤ the provision of a differentiated and appropriate curriculum
➤ the quality of teaching and learning strategies to meet the needs of all the children, to help them achieve the Early Learning Goals, and the range and use of resources (the photocopiable sheet 'Evaluation of teaching and learning' on page 174 and the photocopiable sheet 'Evaluation of the service' on page 175 will help you to do this)
➤ the implementation of key policies such as equal opportunities, special needs and planning
➤ the knowledge and skills of your staff.

Build in ways of reviewing the levels of engagement, quality of planning, teaching and learning, and how you provide the children with a high-quality, broad-based curriculum that supports their development in all key areas, including meeting the Early Learning Goals.

To collect evidence, use videos and analyse them with your staff, talk to parents and carers, make shared observations and regularly track the children and how they engage with each other and the staff, as well as how they cover the Areas of Learning. Make continuous review a key principle of the setting. Encourage your staff to see an inspection as part of the review and evaluation, rather than a fearful experience where the power dynamics are unbalanced and they feel that they are being checked up on and that inspectors want to catch them out and find fault.

The inspection visit

On the day of the inspection, be friendly and welcoming. Remember that inspectors are human and most of them want to be helpful. Arrange for tea and biscuits on arrival. Show them around your setting and explain how the day will work, so that they can identify which activities they may want to observe. Introduce them to parents and staff, and provide relevant information about the setting which can contribute to a smooth inspection: arrival and departure times of the children who attend for sessions; expected visitors; specific needs of children and so on.

OFSTED advises that you carry on as normal on the day of the inspection. This is quite difficult to do because no matter how you reassure staff about the inspection purpose, they will remain on edge, while you will be keen to provide as much evidence as possible to prove how you meet the National Standards. Many inspectors will spend up to four hours with the manager, going through relevant documentation and looking for evidence of the Standards before they do any observation or interviews.

It is worth planning the day very thoroughly so that the staff feel secure and focused, and so that everyone knows what is expected of them. Staff who may be asked about their specific roles can plan to have time available for an interview with the inspector. The manager will also need to make time to go through documentation in the office. This arrangement is obviously difficult for childminders and settings where it is not possible to take time away from the children. Managers in any setting would be advised to avoid other activities or meetings on the inspection day.

The inspection outcome

At the end of the inspection you will receive feedback, both positive and negative. Invite some staff to be present for the feedback session as it will help them to make sense of the whole experience. At the feedback, the inspector will identify any gaps in your compliance with the National Standards and you will have to specify how and by when you will address the issues. The inspector will then set either an 'action' or a 'condition', depending on the seriousness of the situation:

➤ An action states what you have to do and when you should do it by. It is notified to you in the report and a separate letter with an agreed date.
➤ A condition is more serious. It is notified in the report and on the registration certificate. It requires an outcome to be achieved. Once this has been met you will need to contact OFSTED, and an inspector will judge if what you have done meets the National Standards.

A draft report is sent within six weeks of the inspection and you are asked to check it for factual accuracy. You will then be issued with the completed report. You will get a new certificate at this inspection but the setting will not automatically receive new certificates annually, unless there are changes to the setting's registration conditions.

If you have to meet actions or conditions, you are required to write to the Regional Centre identifying what you have done within the agreed time span. This may result in the condition being removed or changed. An inspector may come back to check what you have done, especially if they have not heard from you within the allotted action-plan time. Inspectors can make unannounced visits.

If you do not agree with the judgement

If you do not agree with the final report, you must write to OFSTED within 14 days (see address below). OFSTED has a complaints procedure to help them review and improve the service. Complaints must be made within six months of the incident. You can make a complaint in writing or on the telephone. All complaints are

Helpline
The early years complaints helpline is tel: 0845-601 4772, or you can write to Director of Early Years, OFSTED, Alexandra House, 33 Kingsway, London WC2B 6SE.

investigated and the complainant should receive a written reply explaining what action has been taken within three months. If you are complaining about a duty placed on you by OFSTED, you are obliged to meet that duty while the complaint is being investigated.

The post-inspection plan

To meet any recommendations identified in the report, you will need to make a post-inspection plan. It is advisable to use this as an opportunity to improve the service and, where possible, build it into the annual development plan. There may be resource implications that will require you to find either funds or training opportunities.

Involve the staff in drafting the plan and make sure that they understand why the recommendations were made. Build the plan into your reviewing process. The plans are not required to be sent to OFSTED, but an inspector completing the next visit will want to see how you addressed the recommendations made by the previous inspector. It is also very helpful that parents and other users of the service see how you respond to recommendations. It may be appropriate to involve parents in the planning process, as you may require their help to fund new equipment or make changes to the routine, or support and strengthen home–setting links.

School inspections

Staff working in the maintained sector will be inspected under the requirements of the Primary OFSTED inspection model, where a group of inspectors led by the registered inspector – and including a lay inspector – will spend up to five days at a school, depending on its size.

Among the team of inspectors, there will be an early years OFSTED trained and endorsed inspector who will have experience of children under the age of five and they will write this part of the report. They will usually conduct the interviews with early years staff.

However, other inspectors are also likely to spend time in the early years and they may comment on how the early years team meet the range of Early Learning Goals in the Foundation Stage. The lay inspector often visits the early years team, usually with a strong focus on partnership with parents. The lead inspector will interview the early years co-ordinator to talk about Foundation Stage provision. Other staff and parents may also be informally interviewed. The lay inspector will probably talk to parents and judge how well they are welcomed into the setting. Observations are often made when children arrive and depart.

The lead inspector will want to know about the children's level of attainment on entry to both nursery and Reception classes. Co-ordinators should be prepared to share their analysis of entry profiles, any school assessments and Baseline profiles with them. This is important because you need to show how your provision and work has added value to the children's learning and attainment.

Preparing for inspection

Inspectors are usually checking to see how staff support children to meet the Early Learning Goals, and they will want to see how the team integrate the *Curriculum Guidance for the Foundation Stage* into planning and how the Stepping Stones and Early Learning Goals are used to meet the needs of children of different ages and abilities. They will want to be sure that Reception classes also adhere to the guidance and do not embark on formal work too early.

If you are a new early years manager or co-ordinator, it would be wise to access the most recent OFSTED report either through the Internet or from the head teacher. Read the Foundation Stage section and Part B of the report because this section (which includes management, leadership, the quality of teaching and partnership with parents) will make appropriate reference to early years issues.

Look particularly at the 'key issues' that the school needed to address. These should have formed the basis of the school's post-OFSTED action plan. There may be a direct reference to early years here, for example, 'Improve the provision for outdoor play in Foundation', or the link may be less obvious, for example, 'Improve assessment procedures throughout the school'. Take all this information into account and prepare your personal early years development plan, which should feed into the overall school development plan, possibly as an annex. Inspectors will always want to see what you have done to address the issues of the previous report; being new to the role gives no reprieve!

Getting feedback

During the inspection period all inspectors will offer feedback after observing sessions. This can be given jointly to teaching and support staff if the teacher wishes. Feedback should help you to know what worked well and why in lessons, and also what could be improved and how. Judgements will be made as to whether lessons are unsatisfactory, satisfactory or better, and these will feed into an overall profile on the quality of teaching in the Foundation Stage, and for nursery and Reception classes separately, which will appear in the report.

Co-ordinators should request feedback at the end of the inspection on the quality of their Foundation Stage provision, but this is not automatically given. You may have to wait for the inspectors' formal feedback to the head teacher (probably about 14 days after the inspection ends).

A draft report will be sent to the school about five weeks after inspection and you should check this carefully for accuracy. The head teacher can request minor adjustments and correct any factual errors, but judgements are non-negotiable and cannot be changed.

The final report will arrive six weeks after the inspection took place and a summary must be sent to all parents and carers. The school and governors then have 40 working days to prepare an action plan for OFSTED to show how they will respond to the identified 'key issues'. A summary action plan must also be sent to parents and carers.

If a complaint is necessary, the school has to make this (as early as possible) to the registered inspector and the inspection contractor. If resolution is unsatisfactory, the school can then complain to OFSTED directly. However, OFSTED will only usually deal with matters of a breach of inspection procedures, not with overturning judgements, and officers will always ask whether you have taken up the problem under the contractor's complaints procedure.

NVQ in Management Level 3 links

Elements	Knowledge evidence	Personal competencies
A1.3 Make recommendations for improvements to work activities	A1.3 Analytical techniques Communication Continuous improvement Organisational context	Acting assertively Building teams Communicating
D1.1 Gather required information D1.2 Inform and advise others	D1.1 and D1.2 Analytical techniques Communication Information handling Organisational context	Focusing on results Thinking and taking decisions
C12.1 Plan the work of teams and individuals C12.2 Assess the work of teams and individuals C12.3 Provide feedback to teams and individuals on their work	C12.1 to C12.3 Communication Continuous improvement Information handling Involvement and motivation Monitoring and evaluation Organisational context Planning Working relationships	

Case study

Below is a case study that could be used as a staff-meeting discussion point. Talk about what you would do and why.

You have received a letter from OFSTED giving you an inspection date for a November visit. You are due to be away for three weeks in October and you will be leaving a newly appointed deputy in charge. It is now midway through September. Bring the problem to a staff meeting and ask the team for their response. Use the opportunity to identify and clarify the staff's understanding and expectation of the inspection process and use the National Standards as a teaching tool to explore the staff's knowledge of how, why and where they apply within the setting.

Useful information

➤ Department for Education and Skills (DfES), Sanctuary Buildings, Great Smith Street, London SW1P 3BT. Tel: 0870-001 2345. Website: www.dfes.gov.uk/daycare

➤ Office for Standards in Education (OFSTED), see address on page 125. General enquiry number: 020-7421 6744. Website: www.ofsted.gov.uk

Chapter 10 Developing the service

> ➤ **Planning for development**
> ➤ **Monitoring the service**
> ➤ **What is a quality assurance scheme?**
> ➤ **Quality assurance schemes**
> ➤ **Personal development**

Good management is based on the principle of continuous improvement. Managers need to be able to run the service but also to build in systems for developing it, so that it remains vibrant and dynamic. This will make the provision ready and able to meet the evolving needs of the customers, as well as any planned and unplanned challenges. An organisation that regularly considers how it needs to develop will offer a more accountable, effective and efficient service.

The manager as leader of quality

As a manager, you need to:

➤ form a vision
➤ set realistic and achievable targets
➤ give time targets to meet these objectives
➤ make an operational plan
➤ set an example by leading the team forward
➤ use the lessons of failure
➤ have confidence in yourself and others
➤ be willing to learn and improve
➤ present yourself well
➤ have the courage to take a risk, but think it through before making the leap
➤ avoid asking anyone to do anything that you would not do yourself
➤ get feedback on your own performance and accept the criticism positively
➤ always remember that a leader is only as good as those that he or she leads
➤ aim high, seek constantly to improve your performance and set yourself new and higher targets
➤ take every opportunity to learn and practise new skills.

Planning for development

Running an early years service is an exhausting experience. However, while dealing with the daily routine and responding to the unexpected are very important, building in some thinking and planning time are essential. Therefore, you may consider having a development slot on the staff-meeting agenda perhaps every third meeting, or allocating two staff meetings a year as development meetings. Hold

Manager's tip
Use research rather than trying to guess what customers define as their needs. Ask these questions:

➤ What do our customers want?
➤ What have we done to create the right image?
➤ What have we done in response to their replies?
➤ How do we sell the organisation?
➤ Do we inform our customers of changes?
➤ Do we keep customers fully informed about internal news such as new staff, policies and practices?

When you have reviewed the service, you need to agree on a plan of action to address what to do to ensure improvement. Make the action plan SMART (see page 27), implement the action, then:

➤ check progress
➤ examine success
➤ assess the impact on the service
➤ decide when, how and with whom to share the information
➤ take stock
➤ report and then start again.

Planning is a very helpful process but you need to remain flexible, and help your staff to become flexible, because some eventualities cannot be predicted. These may force you to review and re-examine the plan with possible redirection.

brainstorming meetings where you listen to the staff and ask for ideas. You will then need to call another meeting to agree on how you will act on the ideas. It is very important that the staff be involved in every aspect of the process and that they know what will happen to their ideas. It is very motivating to involve the staff in the action and it may be possible to delegate key roles to the person who suggested specific ideas.

Use these meetings to review the service and:

➤ check that everyone knows the overall aims and objectives of the setting
➤ agree on how you know that you are meeting the objectives, checking last year's action plan, whether the targets have been achieved and whether there are actions still outstanding, and by reviewing the action plan, as it may no longer be appropriate
➤ audit the curriculum provision, access and resources
➤ consider how the children have progressed – is there evidence of concerns about the implementation of the curriculum, children's behaviour, time management for assessment and recording, teaching styles and methods, relationship with parents and links with the community and other agencies that could have an impact on the service?
➤ consider the opportunities available, such as grant funding through the EYDCP, which may in turn encourage you to think about a small project
➤ identify the current stresses faced by the setting
➤ look at how you will solve emerging problems, such as the decaying garden shed or the need to expand baby places
➤ examine what you need to do to keep the setting running effectively
➤ think about the ways in which you will collect feedback and information from children, parents and potential customers. Do you gather information from the staff following training? Do you ask them for their views of the service? Do you use feedback from contract monitoring, OFSTED reports and other information from external moderators or verifiers? Do you check complaints and use that information to influence the development of the organisation? Where possible, it is helpful to put all those comments together on a graph or pictorial chart so that your staff can see at a glance what the service looks like to others.
➤ find out what support your staff may need to meet new challenges
➤ look at what needs to change and whether you will need to introduce a new project
➤ consider whether you could benefit from the help of an adviser or consultant.

Monitoring the service

Monitor your service informally by listening, observing and communicating: a good manager is a visible one. Build in review meetings to allow you to examine the operational issues of the day, check how these may have an impact on the overall service, then resolve any problems highlighted by progress reports. Make monitoring a continual process so that ideas are always encouraged and the purpose of the setting is constantly reinforced.

Sometimes we may lose sight of what we are aiming to provide and our practice may decline because we cut corners to make life easier for ourselves rather than providing a developing and supportive service. For example, we may notice that few fathers get involved in the setting. We could take the view that we are open and willing to see fathers if they come, and so consider it their problem if they do not choose to become involved. However, a reflective service might use this information to review what they do and check that they really offer the kind of information that fathers want, set up displays that actively encourage fathers and so on. The result could be that the service stays the same or that it develops to address the issue, with many positive spin-offs.

Always monitor training. This is an investment in people and is costly in terms of programme fees and staff time. However, if you see the purpose of training as a way of increasing staff competence, developing staff potential and, thereby, improving organisational performance then it makes sense to monitor and evaluate whether it is having the positive effect that you want on the service, staff performance and organisational attitudes.

Monitoring check-list
- ➤ Assess the current situation.
- ➤ Identify strengths and areas for improvement.
- ➤ Involve the staff.
- ➤ Link any improvements to service delivery.
- ➤ Monitor progress and assess the impact on the service.
- ➤ Evaluate progress against priority areas.
- ➤ Check and compare information from staff and customer surveys.
- ➤ Evaluate the impact of training and appraisals.
- ➤ Compare the results achieved from process improvement.

What is a quality assurance scheme?

Improving service quality is a key aim of the National Childcare Strategy, which was launched in May 1998 to support families in the provision of good-quality care. In early years, quality assurance schemes are considered useful tools in the drive to improve quality. Quality improvement or quality assurance schemes raise standards by helping to create an environment of reflective practice and continuous improvement. For this reason, accreditation by a quality scheme has been recognised as a means of improving quality, beyond the minimum standards enforced through registration and inspection procedures.

As part of the National Childcare Strategy, the Government requires 40 per cent of providers to have gained accreditation of an approved quality assurance scheme by 2004. Early Years Development and Childcare Partnerships are actively promoting schemes and are encouraging settings to apply for accreditation. All schemes will need to be accredited by the Government scheme 'Investors in Children'. Investors in Children will award early years settings stars from Level 1 to 3 on the basis of three elements of provision:

- ➤ the result of the OFSTED inspection
- ➤ accreditation by an approved quality assurance scheme
- ➤ the qualifications, training and education of the providers.

The Investors in Children Award is based on research according to which accreditation of a quality assurance scheme, combined with highly qualified and professionally developed staff, is key to good-quality provision. This has been linked to significant improvements in children's linguistic, social and intellectual development.

Quality assurance involves staff in taking a systematic look at the service that they provide and where and how to improve it. Meeting the requirements of a quality assurance programme can enhance your reputation as a provider and an employer. An organisation that has taken part in a quality assurance process can give a message to everyone that it is an organisation that takes its responsibility seriously, and is interested in making sure that the service is continually meeting the needs of the staff and customers.

Most quality assurance systems have a set of accreditation criteria in key areas. The principle that underpins the process is self-evaluation. Therefore, the staff team, together with committee members, trustees, governors and other significant people in the setting, evaluate the service using the accreditation criteria as a framework. They then decide how they will meet the criteria.

The self-assessment process

Taking part in this process is very helpful, especially if you are a new manager, because the criteria can translate vague terms, such as 'improvement', 'development monitoring' and 'review', into actual examples, which is very empowering. Some schemes focus on the childcare and educational aspects of the service, but others look at the main stages of running an organisation which, in turns, helps the manager to see what systems need to be in place or improved and why. The Investors in People (IIP) programme provides a framework in which you can see what needs to be done, to ensure that your staff are supported and developed in an effective and helpful way.

Using a quality assurance process is a good way of motivating all staff (do not forget the cook, cleaner, administrative staff and other support staff) to:

➤ reflect on their strengths, knowledge and expertise
➤ review practice

➤ collect actual information from customers (children, parents and professionals) about what they want from the service
➤ consider new ideas and get a greater view of the part that they play in the whole setting.

Developing quality assurance is a continual process. Demands placed on organisations are continually changing and successful organisations are those that can meet these changes. Eventually, improving quality becomes part of the organisational culture in which everybody is involved and that leads to measurable results over time.

Issues to consider when planning to go through a quality assurance scheme are:

➤ inducting all the staff into the process
➤ agreeing what is evidence
➤ allocating tasks to staff fairly, for example, conducting audits, interviewing parents, undertaking specific observations of children, and so on
➤ if you are using staff members' observations, how much training you will need, especially if using video evidence
➤ time for collecting and collating evidence
➤ how you fit in time to communicate what is happening in an already busy schedule.

Quality assurance schemes

There are a growing number of national quality assurance accreditation schemes, all influenced by research that proves that they improve the service and reputation of an organisation. Generally the schemes, whether management- or occupational-specific, operate through the process of collecting evidence against a set of accreditation criteria, which is then judged by an independent assessor and verified by an approved verification board.

Each scheme produces its own quality assurance pack that varies in cost. There are support systems available through all the lead organisations, but it is worth checking if this incurs extra costs. In addition to such national schemes, EYDCPs and local authorities are developing their own quality assurance schemes, which you can purchase and use. Generally, the quality assurance schemes have a high level of self-assessment and, to be effective, require the co-operation of the whole staff team and management committees.

Examples of quality assurance schemes for early years settings are:

➤ Effective Early Learning (EEL) Programme
➤ Kids' Clubs Network's quality assurance scheme for out-of-school childcare: Aiming High
➤ the Pre-School Learning Alliance's accreditation scheme: Aiming for Quality
➤ the National Day Nurseries Association's accreditation scheme: Quality Counts
➤ the National Childminding Association's Approved Childminding Networks scheme: Children Come First, to accredit childminding networks (formal groups of registered childminders who are assessed, recruited and monitored by a dedicated network co-ordinator).

Personal development

A well-developed service is dependent on a committed, informed and well-developed staff team. The manager has to lead this process and be an effective and inspiring leader. To achieve this, you need to develop your own skills, knowledge and understanding about childcare and education, but also about management. There are plenty of opportunities to do this but you must resist the idea that you cannot justify the time that will be required. Staff are themselves more willing to learn and develop if they see their manager taking the time and energy to do it also. It is sometimes easy to associate development with going on courses, but that is only one way of self-development. Taking a student or becoming an NVQ assessor and developing other people is a very effective way of reviewing your own knowledge and understanding. However, the success of such an approach is determined by a positive and open attitude to self-development.

Many settings engage in action research where they work with an academic organisation to test an idea in the work place. Research is an effective and interesting way of developing new learning as well as understanding and applying it to practice. The manager can benefit in many ways, not least in increased confidence and developing a range of skills and knowledge, from writing a research proposal to presenting the information to interested parties. This approach has been advocated by educationalists throughout the centuries, who have argued that pedagogic practice needs to be continuously adapted and reflected upon if it is to evolve. There is also much to suggest that action research can lead to more effective practice improvement because everyone becomes involved in the process. The EEL Programme had a strong element of action research requiring staff to consider and test solutions to identified challenges.

Attending training, networking, being part of a working group, contributing to magazines and sitting on the EYDCP are all ways of developing yourself. They also offer opportunities for informed professional discussion, which can be motivating and inspiring, especially if you are a lone manager in a setting and cannot share some of the management issues with your staff.

Consider contacting:

➤ the EYDCP for information about training, networking, attending the meetings and other sources of local information.
➤ local colleges, asking them about management and professional development courses
➤ the Council for Awards in Children's Care and Education (CACHE) and City and Guilds about local assessment centres that offer management awards, for example, the NEBSM Introductory Award in Supervisory Management
➤ national training organisations, such as the National Children's Bureau, the National Early Years Network, the National Institute of Education and the National Day Nursery Association
➤ Early Education (formerly BAECE, British Association for Early Childhood Education) for details of their courses
➤ the Universities and Colleges Admissions Service (UCAS) for details of degree courses across the country. If you cannot attend a local college or university, there are distance-learning courses available, for example, from the Open University, the Riverside Early Years Training Centre, the University of Sheffield and Suffolk College.

NVQ in Management Level 3 links

Elements	Knowledge evidence	Personal competencies
A1.3 Make recommendations for improvement to work activities	A1.3, C12.1 to C12.3, F7.1 and F7.2 Analytical techniques Communication	Acting assertively Building teams
C12.1 Plan the work of teams and individuals	Continuous improvement Information handling	Communicating Focusing on results
C12.2 Assess the work of teams and individuals	Involvement and motivation Monitoring and	Influencing others
C12.3 Provide feedback to teams and individuals on their work	evaluation Organisational context Planning Quality management	Searching for information Thinking and taking decisions
F7.1 Audit compliance with quality systems	Working relationships	
F7.2 Follow up quality audits		

Case study

Below is a case study that could be used as a staff-meeting discussion point. Talk about what you would do and why.

You have noticed that the team seem complacent when they are with the children. You feel that there is an element of 'coasting' and that the children are being looked after rather than extended and developed. Going through a quality assurance scheme would be helpful to refocus your team and reviewing the quality of engagement with the children, but the team may be reluctant to take on anything extra and are very unlikely to want to be observed and assessed by an external assessor. How will you find out about the schemes that could help you to address these issues? How will you prepare yourself for this challenge? How will you sell it to your team?

Useful information

➤ National Children's Bureau, Early Childhood Unit, 8 Wakley Street, London EC1V 7QE. Tel: 020-7843 6000. Website: www.ncb.org.uk

Induction for new managers

This form is a guide to help new managers understand what is expected of them and find their way through the management systems. It is a working document and will be a key feature of supervision during the first six months.

Management responsibilities summary

➤ Lead the team.

➤ Ensure that the setting is operating smoothly.

➤ Plan long-, medium- and short-term targets for the development of the service.

➤ Develop and ensure that effective administrative systems including relevant policies and procedures are operational and implemented.

➤ Manage the budget and financial forecasting in line with the setting's planning.

➤ Create and maintain good positive relationships with children, parents, carers, staff and external agencies.

➤ Develop and build a high-performance team, making full use of staff abilities and contributions.

➤ Manage and use time and resources efficiently.

➤ Make properly informed decisions, responding to changing needs and involving staff, ensuring that they are carried out consistently across the setting.

➤ Plan and develop the curriculum.

➤ Solve problems.

➤ Manage change in order to develop and support the whole organisation.

➤ Write relevant reports and correspondence to a high standard

➤ Develop staff in order to support the development of the service and help individuals to achieve their potential.

➤ Maintain an effective level of self-development to ensure that you can effectively manage the service.

➤ Create a service that is underpinned by a principle of continuous review, reflection and evaluation.

Documents to read	Date completed	Comments/questions
Setting operations procedures folder		
Most recent minutes of all meetings		
Parent handbook		
Staff handbook		
Health and safety folder		
Setting annual development plan and OFSTED reports		
Curriculum and planning policies		
Special needs policy		
Children's development records		
Training policy and procedures		
Supervision policy and staff development records		
Admissions procedure		
Settling-in procedure		
Equal opportunities policy		
Child protection policy		
Waiting-list forms		

PHOTOCOPIABLE

Developing staff as individuals

As a manager, how will I demonstrate my understanding of how to develop and maintain staff members?

Targets	Have we agreed on a set of achievable targets in line with relevant plans and recommendations?
Achievement	Can each staff member see how their work contributes to the overall result and positive achievement of the team? Do all the staff have the right skills and knowledge to do their job?
Responsibilities	Is the balance of responsibilities among the team sensible and fair?
Management systems	How do I use my authority to ensure that tasks are completed?
Motivation	Has adequate provision been made for training or retraining, both formally and informally? Are staff encouraged to learn at their own pace? Do I recognise other learning styles?
Recognition	Do I praise and recognise successes? Do I provide constructive criticism?
Development	Can staff see the chance for development?
Performance	Is staff progress and development regularly reviewed?
Time/attention	Do I spend enough time/attention listening, developing and supporting staff members?
Complaints and concerns	Are complaints and concerns promptly addressed?
Supervision	How am I using supervision?

Building and maintaining the team

Objective	How will I share my vision with the team?
Standards	How will they know what standards of performance I expect?
Responsibility	How will I explain the consequences if these standards are not constantly maintained?
Team-building	What opportunities can I develop to build up teamwork into each task? How will I develop team spirit?
Balance	Am I fair to all staff? Am I consistent in the way that I apply the rules of the setting?
Involvement	Have I created an environment that encourages ideas and suggestions from the team?
Motivation	How do I encourage and praise the team? Am I sure I do or do I just *think* I do?

Manager's handbook   *early years* **training & management**

Managing every day in the setting

Do I demonstrate an ability to manage the following tasks? How? What action do I need?

The children are cared for and educated within a stimulating, happy and supportive environment following the philosophical principles of the setting.

How could I prove it?

What do I need to do to be able to?

The development needs of the children are met within the framework of planned activities that also enable learning to take place within an anti-discriminatory environment. This could include:
➤ provision of activities to aid current learning needs of children
➤ ability to respond appropriately to the initiatives demonstrated by the children
➤ ability to focus the children's attention and make the most of learning opportunities
➤ ability to make the most of young children's curiosity
➤ ability to ensure equal opportunities across the curriculum
➤ positive demonstration that all the children and other cultures are respected
➤ provision of opportunities for first-hand experimentation/exploration/observation/discussion.

How could I prove it?

What do I need to do to be able to?

Ensure that staff supervise, observe and respond to the children. This could include:
➤ ability to oversee the implementation of health and safety
➤ ability to organise and direct the children
➤ ability to support staff to define and implement safe boundaries and expectations with and for the children
➤ ability to manage your own activity while keeping an overview of the rest of the activities
➤ being supportive of staff, particularly when they are dealing with complex situations and difficult or challenging decisions.

How could I prove it?

What do I need to do to be able to?

To ensure that staff engage in meaningful and regular dialogue with parents, carers and other relevant professionals. This could include:

➤ ability to form effective, warm relationships with the children
➤ willingness and ability to make contact with parents
➤ ability to create links with other agencies, submit reports and contribute to meetings where appropriate
➤ initiate and maintain regular open and constructive communication with staff members
➤ keep up-to-date, accessible, properly filed records
➤ make assessments of the children's needs and record appropriately
➤ keep the children's developmental records up to date and well written, with relevant evidence
➤ organise parents' evenings and newsletters
➤ put up curriculum displays for parents that are up to date and clear
➤ ensure that the waiting list is kept updated and that every effort is made to fill vacancies.

How could I prove it?

What do I need to do to be able to?

Ensure effective teamwork. This could include:

➤ develop good professional relationships in each member of staff
➤ ability to identify strengths and weaknesses of team members and support their development through training and development plans
➤ ability to offer support guidance and direction to all staff members
➤ organise regular staff meetings with clear agenda and minutes recorded with a clear action plan
➤ delegate fairly and constructively to team members, giving the team appropriate support and information to enable them to respond satisfactorily
➤ motivate staff through a variety of means, including delegating areas of responsibility and planning a training and development programme
➤ deal with conflicts and poor performance fairly and sensitively, ensuring that evidence is collected and recorded
➤ work within the personnel policies.

How could I prove it?

What do I need to do to be able to?

Manager's handbook

To maintain budgets, you need:
➤ the ability to ensure that budgets are kept updated and properly recorded
➤ to complete regular financial updates.

How could I prove it?

What do I need to do to be able to?

Maintain an efficient office by:
➤ setting up effective office administration systems
➤ using a computer where possible to ensure effective maintenance of files and records
➤ completing the relevant administration tasks and submit the paperwork on time
➤ completing weekly staff-for-the-week forms and monthly planners
➤ responding to tasks within the time span agreed
➤ contributing to the formulation and review of policies and procedures
➤ dealing with outgoing and incoming mail
➤ supporting staff to write well-presented reports for outside agencies
➤ ensuring that staff are fully aware of office systems
➤ completing induction programmes for new staff
➤ providing regular supervision to all staff
➤ maintaining all records as required.

How could I prove it?

What do I need to do to be able to?

NVQ in Management Level 3 links

Before beginning the NVQ in Management Level 3, check how you identify where, when and why you use the following skills on both a daily and more specific basis, then show your assessor how you apply them for each unit.

Units	Personal competencies	Do you do this now?	Where is the evidence?
C1, C4, C12 C1, C4, D1 D1, C12 D1, C15 C7, C9, C15 C7, C9, C15 C12	**Acting assertively** Take personal responsibility for making things happen. Say no to unreasonable requests. Take a leading role in initiating action and making decisions. Act in an assured and unhesitating manner when faced with a challenge. State your own position and views clearly in conflict situations. Maintain your beliefs, commitment and efforts in spite of set-backs and opposition. Take control of situations and events.		
C7, C15 C7, C15	**Behaving ethically** Comply with legislation, industry regulation, professional and organisational codes. Show integrity and fairness in decision-making.		
A1, C4, C9, C12 A1, C12, C15 A1, D1 C9, C12 C4, D1, C12 C4, C9, C12, C15 C4, C9, C12 C4, D1, C12, C15 C4, D1, C12, C15 C9, C12 C9, C12 C9, C12, C15 C9, C12, C15 C12, C15 C12, C15 C12, C15	**Building teams** Keep others informed about plans and progress. Clearly identify what is required of others. Invite others to contribute to planning and organising work. Actively build relationships with others. Make time available to support others. Provide feedback designed to improve people's future performance. Show respect for the views and actions of others. Show sensitivity to the needs and feelings of others. Set objectives which are both achievable and challenging. Evaluate and enhance people's capacity to do their jobs. Encourage and stimulate others to make the best use of their abilities. Use power and authority in a fair and equitable manner. Check individuals' commitment to a specific course of action. Use a variety of techniques to promote morale and productivity. Identify and resolve causes of conflict or resistance.		
A1,B1,C1,C4,D1,C9 A1, B1, C4, D1, C7, C9, C12, F7 A1, D1, C9 B1, C4, D1, C7, C9, C12, C15 C1, D1, C7, C9, C15, F7 C1, D1, C7, C9, C12, C15 D1, C7, C9, C12, C15, F7 C9	**Communicating** Identify the information needs of listeners. Adopt communication styles appropriate to listeners and situations, including selecting an appropriate time and place. Use a variety of media and communication aids to reinforce points and maintain interest. Listen actively, ask questions, clarify points and rephrase others' statements to check mutual understanding. Encourage listeners to ask questions or rephrase statements to clarify their understanding. Modify communication in response to feedback from listeners. Confirm listeners' understanding through questioning and interpretation of non-verbal signs. Present difficult ideas and problems in ways that promote understanding.		

PHOTOCOPIABLE

■SCHOLASTIC

Manager's handbook

Units	Personal competencies	Do you do this now?	Where is the evidence?
A1 A1 A1, B1, C1 A1, B1, C1, C15 A1, C15 B1, C1 C15 C15	**Focusing on results** Actively seek to do things better. Use change as an opportunity for improvement. Tackle problems and take advantage of opportunities as they arise. Maintain a focus on objectives. Monitor quality of work and progress against plans. Prioritise objectives and schedule work to make the best use of time and resources. Establish and communicate high expectations of performance, including setting an example to others. Continually strive to identify and minimise barriers to excellence.		
D1 D1, C7, F7 C7 C7	**Influencing others** Use a variety of means to influence others. Present yourself positively to others. Create and prepare strategies for influencing others. Understand the culture of your organisation and act to work within it or influence it.		
C1 C1 C1 C1 C4 C4 C4	**Managing self** Take responsibility for meeting own learning and development needs. Seek feedback on performance to identify strengths and weaknesses. Learn from your own mistakes and those of others. Change behaviour where needed as a result of feedback. Accept personal comments or criticism without becoming defensive. Remain calm in difficult or uncertain situations. Handle others' emotions without becoming personally involved in them.		
D1 D1, C7 D1, C7 D1, C7 D1, C7 C7	**Searching for information** Establish information networks to search for and gather relevant information. Make best use of existing sources of information. Seek information from multiple sources. Challenge the validity and reliability of sources of information. Push for concrete information in an ambiguous situation. Actively encourage the free exchange of information.		
B1 B1, C1, D1 B1, C4, D1 B1, C1, C4, D1, C7, C9, C12, F7 C1, C7, C9, C12, F7 C1, F7 C4 C7 C9, F7 F7	**Thinking and taking decisions** Make use of, and reconcile, a variety of perspectives when making sense of a situation. Produce a variety of solutions before taking a decision. Produce your own ideas from experience and practice. Take decisions which are realistic for the situation. Break processes down into tasks and activities. Identify implications, consequences or causal relationships in a situation. Focus on facts, problems and solutions when handling an emotional situation. Identify patterns or meaning from events and data which are not obviously related. Use your own experience and evidence from others to identify problems and understand situations. Identify a range of elements in and perspectives on a situation.		

Nursery Officer job description

Post title: Nursery Officer   **Responsible to: Manager**

Objectives

To plan, organise and deliver activities and create learning experiences for a group of children aged between two and five years old (or six months to five years). To work within an anti-discriminatory and inclusive environment and support the team to facilitate the all-round development of all children, enabling them to reach their full potential.

Key responsibilities

➤ To plan and organise activities and opportunities that extend learning.

➤ To produce accurate and effective observations so as to assess the children's progress and the effectiveness of the learning environment.

➤ To work to support the development of the children within an early years curriculum framework.

➤ To manage the children's behaviour and routines in line with the setting's policies and guidelines.

➤ To work within a key-worker system.

➤ To maintain objective, accurate and up-to-date records that identify the children's individual needs, abilities and progress, and use these as a focus for future planning.

➤ To work in partnership with parents and carers at all times.

➤ To work within the setting's health and safety guidelines and undertake specific tasks related to the safety and hygiene of the children and the nursery.

➤ To work within the setting's child protection procedures.

➤ To work within the setting's equal opportunities policy.

➤ To share tasks necessary as part of the general upkeep, tidiness and cleanliness of the nursery, and which contribute to the general well-being of the team.

➤ To plan and participate in outings and trips and be aware of additional responsibilities for the children's safety that these necessitate.

➤ To take part in and support fund-raising activities.

➤ To participate in and contribute to regular staff meetings, supervision (with manager) and training so as to improve skills and knowledge and develop a positive attitude that enhances practice.

➤ To assist in the support and supervision of students in the nursery and complete relevant training to ensure that this is of high quality.

➤ To undertake specific roles and responsibilities within the nursery that will involve attending meetings, cascading information and receiving relevant training.

➤ To undertake any other tasks, as requested by the management team, that are necessary for the smooth running of the nursery and the welfare of the children in its care.

PHOTOCOPIABLE

Person specification for a nursery officer

Name: L. Friedrich   Ref: 2   Outcome: Appoint

Essential criteria		A = assess from application I = assess from interview	Met	Not met	Comments
1.	A	NNEB, NVQ Level 3 or BTEC (Childcare) or other qualification as recognised within the childcare framework.			NVQ 3 original certificate checked.
2.	A/I	Willingness to improve and apply written skills sufficient to enable recording of professional reports.			Clear application form. Understood importance of good presentation.
3.	A/I	Demonstrates knowledge and understanding of child development.			Limited knowledge of babies but good understanding of two- and three-year-olds.
4.	A/I	Demonstrates knowledge of early years curriculum and understanding of its purpose in planning.			Could name the ELGs and expand on some. Poor understanding of KUW.
5.	A/I	Demonstrates understanding of the key-worker role and responsibility for children's developmental records.			Currently key worker. Referenced attachment theory. Recognised difficulty of managing key-worker system.
6.	A/I	Demonstrates ability, and understands need, to manage children's behaviour.			Very positive approach. Considered that she might be at fault for having unreal expectations or providing boring activities.
7.	A/I	Demonstrates understanding of need for working in partnership with parents and carers.			Currently does parent workshops.
8.	A/I	Commitment to equal opportunities and understanding of anti-discrimination practices.			Bit stuck on festivals but understood about diversity and special needs.
9.	A/I	Demonstrates knowledge of health and safety: indoors, outdoors and on trips.			Limited. Could list things but forgot all about recording and prevention.
10.	A/I	Demonstrates knowledge of nursery hygiene.			Made reference to toilet procedures and use of gloves.
11.	A/I	Demonstrates willingness to work within and understand the importance of child protection procedures.			No real experience but knew about the policy.
12.	A/I	Demonstrates willingness and ability to contribute to the well-being of the team.			Good understanding about team dynamics. Talked about storming and re-forming, and about active participation.

PHOTOCOPIABLE

		Essential criteria	Met	Not met	Comments
13.	A/I	Demonstrates understanding of the concept of reliability in a nursery.			Good time-keeping according to reference. Eight days sick, single episodes. Very weak.
14.	A/I	Demonstrates understanding of the need to adapt and meet the challenges of change.			Example of moving to London and coping with agency work.
15.	A/I	Demonstrates understanding of the requirements of being a professional team member.			Friendly, calm, willing, pull your weight, listen to others and be sensitive (good suggestions).
16.	A/I	Demonstrates understanding of need for and commitment to maintain confidentiality.			Only in conjunction with child protection
17.	A/I	Demonstrates ability to respond appropriately to unexpected circumstances.			No example.
18.	A/I	Willingness to take on and develop specific roles within the nursery.			Recognised this as a learning opportunity. Wants to be HSO.
19.	A/I	Willingness to participate in, contribute to and learn from meetings and in-service training days.			Said so and described them as motivating.
20.	A/I	Awareness of the concept of self-development and demonstrated ability to find and use opportunities, both internal and external.			Understood that training is more important than courses and that learning to present and participate in meetings is a very helpful learning opportunity. Also said that she learns from the children. Example of dinosaurs.
21.	I	Good oral communication skills (ability to communicate effectively with children, parents and carers, other professionals and colleagues).			Clear and articulate. Body language animated.
		Desirable criteria			**Comments**
1.	A	Written skills sufficient to enable the recording of professional reports.			Needs help with grammar and spelling.
2.	A/I	To speak/write a second language as well as English.			Portuguese.
3.	A/I	To have an additional creative skill that can be used with the children.			Plays the guitar.

This form provides evidence of the candidate's ability to meet the required criteria of the job. At this stage there can be no 'not mets'. The panel has to come to the conclusion that the evidence is sufficient for them to agree either to appoint or not. The evidence will be the source of feedback to unsuccessful candidates.

Probation form for nursery staff

Name _____ Setting _____

Job title _____ Manager _____

Knowledge and skills Understanding and applying the early years curriculum	Comments and agreed targets
☐ Demonstrated knowledge of child development.	
☐ Asks questions and seeks advice when necessary.	
☐ Works within curriculum policies.	
☐ Understands and can complete long-, medium- and short-term planning records.	
☐ Can articulate what is meant by anti-discriminatory practice and demonstrates this in practice.	
☐ Complies with the child protection procedures when necessary.	
☐ Completes relevant nursery records correctly and on time.	
☐ Co-operates with other professionals as appropriate.	
☐ Demonstrates the ability to work in partnership with parents and carers.	
Knowledge and skills Health and safety	**Comments and agreed targets**
☐ Has good health and safety standards, which are reflected in work around the nursery.	
☐ Can apply the health and safety policy correctly where appropriate.	

☐ Co-operates with health and safety initiatives within the nursery (such as risk assessment).	
☐ Is aware of his/her responsibility for safety of the children, adults and staff.	
☐ Pays close attention to the children and supervises them correctly.	
☐ Comment and agreed targets	

Knowledge and skills Communication skills	**Comments and agreed targets**
☐ Communicates effectively with adults.	
☐ Communicates effectively with the children.	
☐ Positive communication with parents and carers.	
☐ Appropriate sharing and accepting information from other professionals.	
☐ Keeps clear, well-written, grammatically correct records.	
☐ Applies confidentiality reasonably and appropriately.	
☐ Knowledge of and interaction with key children.	
☐ Shares information with and communicates information to the manager.	
☐ Shares in the development of the team.	
☐ Participates in the creation of displays.	
☐ Contributes to the planning of activities both orally and by completing relevant written records.	
☐ Responds positively to challenges.	
☐ Resolves differences quickly and in a way that will mend fences.	

Knowledge and skills Work as a team member	Comments and agreed targets
☐ Punctuality.	
☐ Reliability.	
☐ Adheres to the setting's policies and procedures.	
☐ Accepts supervision and contributes to the process.	
☐ Participates in staff meetings.	
☐ Attends relevant training and shares information with team colleagues.	
☐ Works within the equal opportunities policy of the setting.	

Overall outcome

☐ Satisfactory performance of staff member over the past six months. The outcome takes into account the level of experience and knowledge that the staff member has brought with them to the job and the time that it takes for a new staff member to become accustomed to the workings of the setting.

☐ Performance is unsatisfactory and does not meet the standards required within the setting. This outcome must only be used where clear evidence is available to indicate where the individual does not meet standards. Specific action must have been taken to ensure that they understood the standards and were supported to meet them.

Do you wish to confirm his/her appointment?   Yes/No

Do you wish to extend the probationary period?   Yes/No   If yes, please specify the period:

_____

Manager's signature _____   Staff member's signature _____

Date _____

Record of staff attendance on training courses

For display in your setting and to be filled in by staff as they complete training. This information is also required by OFSTED.

Name of staff member	Training attended	Date	Information in personal development file?	How is training information shared?	Signed by manager

PHOTOCOPIABLE

After-course questionnaire

This form has been designed to collect your immediate reaction to the training.

Training programme title _____

Date _____

Tutor _____

Participant's name _____

1. How did you rate the training overall?

   Poor   1   2   3   4   5   Excellent

2. What were your learning objectives prior to taking part in the training?

   _____

3. To what extent were your objectives met?

   Poor   1   2   3   4   5   Excellent

4. How would you rate the training in terms of:

   ➤ content   Poor   1   2   3   4   5   Excellent

   ➤ format   Poor   1   2   3   4   5   Excellent

   ➤ presentation   Poor   1   2   3   4   5   Excellent

5. What is your assessment of the trainer(s)?

   Poor   1   2   3   4   5   Excellent

6. Which aspect of the training did you find most useful?

   _____

7. What else did you think the training could cover?

   _____

8. How and when do you think you will use what you learned on the training in the work place?

   _____

   _____

Any further comments

_____

_____

Learning-impact evaluation form

This form has been designed to collect information that shows any change that you have made to existing skills, knowledge and attitude, any new learning and how you have implemented this in your practice.

Attendee _____

Training course title _____

Date _____ Tutor _____

Dear staff member

You have recently completed the (*state the course*). Our policy is to carry out follow-up questionnaires to staff who have attended the course within 12 weeks. This is because it has been found that if some aspects of a new skill learned on a training course are not applied within 12 weeks, the learning is likely to be forgotten. We use the questionnaire to find out:

➤ if the course was effective
➤ if you have used your new learning in the setting
➤ if you could name one change you have made to your practice since completing the course.

I would be grateful, therefore, if you would answer the following three questions and return the form to me by the end of (*give date*).

1. What were your learning objectives prior to taking part in the course?

_____

2. Which did you learn on the course?

_____

3. How and what learning have you applied in the work place since completing the course?

_____

Any further comments

_____

Thank you. Please file a copy in your personal development file.

Date _____

PHOTOCOPIABLE

◗SCHOLASTIC

Manager's handbook  *early years* **training & management**

Supervision policy

Introduction

We believe that the provision of a high-quality service can only be achieved through good practice from competent and confident staff. In order for this to happen, it is necessary for staff members to be provided with direction, support, learning opportunities and regular supervision.

Supervision is a formal process in which the workload and performance of each member of the team is consistently evaluated and reviewed, in order to raise standards and facilitate learning and change.

This supervision policy identifies the practice, principles and process of supervision within our setting.

Supervision objectives

➤ Create an atmosphere of shared trust, honesty and good communication.
➤ Ensure that the staff members provide an efficient and effective service.
➤ Help staff to grow and develop professionally.
➤ Maximise staff knowledge and skills.
➤ Encourage the development of a reflective practitioner.
➤ Support staff members within the work context.
➤ Enable staff members to feel good about their jobs.
➤ Agree and assess learning and career development.

The purpose of supervision

Supervision is not just a key means of supporting and developing staff, it is also a very effective way of influencing the quality of the service that you provide. Managers need to use supervision to:

➤ help staff to understand their roles and responsibilities in the setting
➤ support staff in continuing to learn and develop professionally in order that they may cope with the changing demands of the work place
➤ enable staff to initiate fresh ways of looking at their practice
➤ encourage staff to become effective and positive members of the team
➤ support staff in evaluating their progress and reflect on their practice
➤ celebrate staff members' achievements
➤ support staff in managing negative stress and establishing a useful balance between work and personal life
➤ give constructive feedback
➤ identify training and development opportunities.

The supervision process

In order to offer supervision, managers need to have good interpersonal and communication skills as well as a thorough knowledge of their job. They also need to be able to manage the supervision process, setting clear boundaries, separating their own values, attitudes and beliefs from others', while remaining sensitive to those of their staff members.

PHOTOCOPIABLE

Managers must endeavour to help their staff get the most from their experience in the setting. Creating a formal process is a useful starting-point.

➤ Supervision is a planned and formal process.
➤ Staff need to sign a supervision contract that states that they are prepared to work within the policy and contribute to the process.
➤ Managers and staff will prepare for supervision and consider what needs discussing in advance.
➤ An agenda will be prepared to remind staff of the key areas of their work. This could include key children, training, implementing policies and procedures, relationship with colleagues, new interests and so on.
➤ The meetings will be on a one-to-one basis and take place every eight weeks.
➤ Managers will ensure that a supervision session is conducted in a positive way. Staff will be encouraged to ask questions and have their views considered. Supervision is ultimately a key factor in the development of the reflective practitioner.
➤ Supervision will be recorded and both parties will have a copy of the records.
➤ At the end of each supervision session, managers and staff members will agree on SMART targets and record this agreed action.
➤ Records will be stored in a safe place and, if needed for other purposes such as a disciplinary hearing, will be used within policies and procedures. Records will be kept within the principles of the Data Protection Act 1998.
NB Each setting needs to agree on how long to keep supervision records and what to do with them if the staff transfer within the company.

Roles and responsibilities
Supervisors have the responsibility to:

➤ hold regular supervision at least every eight weeks
➤ encourage the supervisee to identify and meet their job-related training and development, including induction
➤ make staff aware of development opportunities open to them
➤ plan and prepare supervision in advance
➤ review staff progress to inform the training and development plan
➤ ensure that all supervision records are complete
➤ keep all records secure and private.

Supervisees have the right to:

➤ ask questions about how things are done and what is expected and receive a clear and informative reply
➤ be given appropriate support for all aspects of work undertaken
➤ have their viewpoints listened to and considered
➤ have achievement and consistent good practice recognised and encouraged
➤ discuss and complete a training and development plan
➤ be informed clearly and constructively with specific examples if there are areas where work is not satisfactory.

Conclusion

This policy applies to all staff. It is the responsibility of line managers to ensure that supervision is carried out within this policy. It is also worth remembering that good supervision depends on:

➤ mutual trust
➤ honesty
➤ good communication
➤ mutual support
➤ clear boundaries.

I the undersigned have read and understood the contents of my supervision contract and agree to work within the content and spirit of the policy so as to make best use of the supervision experience.

Signed by supervisee _____

Signed by supervisor _____

Date _____

Supervision review form

This form has been designed to help staff identify key targets for development throughout the year. The manager and the staff member will agree on them in supervision. The targets will be reviewed throughout the year and consolidated in the annual training and development review.

The plans provide positive ways to help the manager and staff member to focus on news areas of development and will help new staff to identify and explore the more complex aspects of their job tasks and responsibilities.

Key targets for development	Training and support needed to reach targets	Target start dates	How will you know when you have achieved the target?	Review date and action

PHOTOCOPIABLE

Manager's handbook

Staff annual development appraisal

Name _____

Job title _____

Date of appraisal _____

Length of time in post _____

All training courses attended this year, including twilight, distance-learning and evening courses:

Date	Course title	Course structure (internal/external/workshop/twilight/distance learning/evening)	Outcome (award/certificate and so on)

What were your key learning and development achievements this year?

Review of the achievements that you have listed in the previous section

What was most challenging about your achievements? Why?

What was the most satisfying aspect of your achievements? Why?

How have you applied your new skills/knowledge at work?

What support/resources helped you to achieve this?

Annual personal development plan

Complete this form in advance of your appraisal meeting. Use your comments as the focus for the meeting and agree on new targets for your personal development this year. This form will be kept with your supervision notes and a personal copy must be filed in your personal development file.

What must you do to gain the skills and knowledge you think you need to achieve these targets?

What specific training courses do you think would help you to achieve these targets?

How will your development plan benefit your setting? Can you link it to the setting's development plan and external issues in early years?

What new support or resources would be useful to you?

Setting philosophy

➤ We believe that care and education are integral.

➤ We believe that children are best supported when parents and staff work together.

➤ Our curriculum is play-based, because we believe that children learn best through supported play experiences.

➤ We believe that children need to be respected in order to respect.

➤ We believe that the learning environment must be planned to ensure that children are provided with rich and stimulating experiences, to build on what they already know and can do.

➤ We will support the children to use the resources and the environment in a way that will develop their independence and problem-solving skills.

➤ We will help the children to develop positive relationships with other children and adults.

➤ In order to foster the children's positive sense of self and self-esteem, we will ensure that the experiences, family background, interests, abilities and cultural heritage will be positively celebrated and reflected across the service.

➤ We believe that it is very important to provide staff with training and development opportunities so that they, in turn, can provide the children with effective learning and teaching.

➤ We work hard to be part of the local community, accessing local resources so that the children have a sense of connection and belonging.

➤ We endeavour to network with other professionals for the benefit of the service.

These principles apply to every part of our service.

Ideas to try at home

Dear Parents

We are learning about .... at the moment. Please could you remind your child about what he or she is learning in the nursery when playing, talking, shopping, commuting, getting dressed, having breakfast and so on? A little encouragement is usually the most effective way to help children. Whatever you do, have fun together!

Thank you.

Areas of Learning	Activities

Induction programme for a new SENCO

The following programme identifies the responsibilities of a staff member undertaking the role of special educational needs co-ordinator (SENCO). Use the form as a way of getting to know what the SENCO does. Your manager will go through the form with you, also checking how you can gain the knowledge and understanding necessary to meet the requirements of being a SENCO. You may find it helpful to talk to the previous SENCO or to a colleague in another setting who already fulfils this role.

SENCO induction	Comments and questions	Read and understood
Where do I start? ➤ Where is the special educational needs (SEN) file? ➤ Do I have a SENCO role description? ➤ Do I need to keep a special needs register? ➤ Do I have the contact details for the main support services: 　• Social Services Department 　• Speech and Language Therapy Service 　• Child Development Service 　• Educational Psychology and Pupil Support Services 　• Special Needs Unit at the Local Education Department? ➤ Does the whole team know that I am the SENCO? ➤ Do I know how and when to share special needs information with the team? ➤ Does the SENCO have a budget?		
Policy implementation ➤ Is the SEN file up to date? ➤ Does it have the relevant information? How can I check? ➤ Have I read and do I understand my responsibilities for the special needs policy? ➤ Do I understand my responsibilities for the implementation of other policies with regards to children with SEN such as: 　• personal, social and emotional policy 　• planning policy 　• equal opportunities policy 　• all curriculum policies? ➤ Is the whole team aware of its responsibility for the provision of a suitable curriculum for SEN children? ➤ Do I need to work with the manager to plan induction for any new staff, students and agency workers?		

PHOTOCOPIABLE

SENCO induction	Comments and questions	Read and understood
Individual education plans (IEPs) ➤ Can I complete an IEP correctly? ➤ Where are the files? ➤ Am I fully aware of my responsibility to share information and co-ordinate the SEN process? ➤ Am I certain that every key worker with an SEN child knows the process of Early Action and Early Action Plus? ➤ What will I do to help all staff to complete IEPs? ➤ Do they know how to write SMART statements? ➤ Where are IEP curriculum targets displayed? ➤ Have SEN children been planned for during the topic planning meeting? ➤ Before I start an IEP, do I know where I can find all the information that I will need? ➤ Do I understand my responsibility for involving the parents or carers in the SEN process?		
IEP reviews ➤ Are the reviews completed every six weeks? ➤ If the advisory teacher visited in the morning, would she find up-to-date and well-recorded IEPs? ➤ In helping staff to complete IEPs, have I identified training needs? ➤ Do I understand my responsibility for involving the parents or carers in the review process?		
Statutory statementing process ➤ Am I fully aware of my responsibility with regards to the statementing process? ➤ Am I certain that every key worker with an SEN child also knows the process? ➤ Do I understand my responsibility for involving the parents or carers in the review process?		
OFSTED reports ➤ When was the setting last inspected by OFSTED? ➤ Did the inspector make any recommendations regarding SEN provision? ➤ Have all the recommendations that were made been implemented? If not, do we know why not and what measures have been taken?		

PHOTOCOPIABLE

SENCO induction	Comments and questions	Read and understood
Staff-meeting minutes ➤ Is SEN a regular item on the staff meeting agenda? ➤ Do the minutes make recommendations and/or action points about SEN issues so that staff are clear about their responsibilities? ➤ Have I reported back to the meeting all issues arising from SENCO meetings? ➤ Have I have taken note of recommendations from staff meetings and progressed them as appropriate?		
Record-keeping and monitoring ➤ Is the SEN file in order and up to date? ➤ Have I done the IEP monitoring? ➤ Are the IEP records adequate, properly dated and signed? Would they make sense to someone who did not know the child? ➤ Do I need to agree with my manager on sufficient time to undertake all tasks identified?		
Keeping up to date ➤ Is a copy of the new *Code of Practice* in the setting? ➤ Have I read it and do I understand the information? ➤ Am I alert to opportunities for obtaining information on the role of the SENCO (such as leaflets from libraries)? ➤ Where else might I go if I want information on the role of the SENCO?		

Manager's handbook  early years *training & management*

Special educational needs policy

Introduction	Set the context. Consider relevant legislation and explain why a policy is needed. Use the introduction to set the context, for example, the new *Code of Practice*.
Policy aims	➤ To recognise and support the underlying principles of the Care Standards Act 2000, the Children Act 1989, the Education Acts (Amendment) Act 2000 and the Special Educational Needs and Disability Act 2001, as well as the regulations of the *Code of Practice*. ➤ To offer a professional service in order to provide the best possible quality care and education for children with special educational needs. ➤ To provide a calm but stimulating inclusive learning environment, through access and positive staff attitudes, removing where possible barriers to learning. ➤ To make the best possible use of resources, both within the setting and beyond, to prepare the children to become active and valued members of the community. ➤ To ensure that staff are informed of their duty towards children with special educational needs, operate within the SEN policy and procedures, and are fully aware of the procedures for identifying, assessing and making provision for children with special needs. ➤ To work towards continual improvement of the service by regularly monitoring and evaluating the provision, in order to achieve the best possible approach, through a range of resources, support and training opportunities.
How to implement the policy	➤ Ensure that all staff understand and can implement the special educational needs policy. ➤ Ensure that all staff understand their roles and responsibilities. ➤ Appoint a special educational needs co-ordinator. ➤ Develop relevant records and keep these maintained. ➤ Provide relevant training for all staff. ➤ Review the policy and procedures regularly. ➤ Work in partnership with parents, carers and other professionals.

The role of the staff in implementing the policy:
The manager
	➤ The role of the **manager** is to oversee the day-to-day implementation of the SEN policy. This requires working closely with the SENCO and supporting them to carry out the role and responsibilities by:
	  • responding to their concerns
	  • attending the meeting arranged by them to discuss initial concerns
	  • ensuring that all team members are fully informed of their duty towards children with special educational needs, operate within the SEN policy, and are fully aware of the procedures for identifying, assessing and making provision for children with special needs.

The key worker	➤ The **key worker** has responsibility for gathering information about the child and contributing towards an initial assessment of the child's special educational needs. The key worker provides special help within the curriculum

Manager's handbook

	framework, exploring ways in which increased differentiation of the nursery curriculum might better meet the needs of the individual child. He or she also provides the child with an opportunity to share their feelings about the learning needs. The key worker monitors and reviews the child's progress, and works co-operatively with the SENCO and the child's parents or carers throughout the whole process.
The special educational needs co-ordinator	➤ For the role of the **special educational needs co-ordinator**, see the photocopiable sheets 'Induction programme for a new SENCO' on pages 162–164.
How to decide when a child needs Early Action	➤ Seek advice from your special educational needs co-ordinator if you suspect that a a child: • makes little or no progress, even when teaching approaches are particularly targeted to improve their identified area of weakness • continues working at levels significantly below those of children of a similar age in certain areas • presents persistent emotional and/or behavioural difficulties that are not ameliorated by the behaviour-management techniques usually employed in the setting • has sensory or physical problems and continues to make little or no progress, despite the provision of personal aids or equipment. ➤ If appropriate, draw up an individual educational plan (IEP).
When do you review the IEP?	➤ If you suspect further problems, consult the SENCO and complete a review of the IEP. ➤ Check: Has progress been made? What are the parents' views? Is there need for more information or advice about the child?
When do you use Early Years Action Plus?	➤ Early Years Action Plus is when external support services become involved. These services may be involved to give advice with IEPs, provide more specialist assessment, give advice on the use of new or specialist strategies or materials and in some cases provide support for particular activities. All this will depend on what is available from the Local Authority. ➤ If the child is making little progress, the SENCO and key worker pull together all known information about the child, including any involvement with outside agencies. ➤ Talk to the parents or carers to get additional information and keep them involved throughout. ➤ If the parents agree, the SENCO can seek the advice of relevant professionals ,such as the Early Years Partnership Advisory team. ➤ Take account of special issues such as children and parents with English as an additional language. ➤ Use all the above information to write your Early Years Action Plus plan.

■SCHOLASTIC

Manager's handbook
early years
training & management

How and when do you make a request for statutory assessment?	➤ If a child is not making progress through Early Years Action Plus, the setting may need, in consultation with the parents and any external agencies already involved, to consider whether a statutory multi-disciplinary assessment may be necessary. Parents, schools and settings can make a request to the LEA for a statutory assessment. Currently, non-maintained nurseries can only make a request for assessment if the child is four or five years. ➤ Insert information about this process as laid down by the Education Department Special Needs Unit.
Statements for children under compulsory school age but over two years	Insert relevant guidance.
Statements for children under two years	➤ Statements are rare for children under two years. The LEA needs to consider the individual child's needs. The procedures are not specified in the legislation. The LEA needs to take account of voluntary arrangements and parental views, but a request for assessment may indicate that the arrangements are not sufficient. When meeting the needs of children under two, the LEA should consider home-based services such as Portage and peripatetic services. ➤ Insert key information for action.
Special educational provision for children under compulsory school age	➤ Where a child's educational needs appear to be sufficiently severe or complex as to require attention for much of the child's school life, or where the evidence points to the need for specialist early intervention that cannot be provided in the current setting, the LEA is likely to conclude that an assessment is necessary. ➤ Insert guidance on what to do.
Preliminary form ('worry form')	Devise a form that collects information about the child at an early stage of concern. Write in the policy what happens at this stage and who is responsible. Collect all relevant information on the form and use simple headings such as 'Why am I worried?' and 'What action shall I take?'.
Form 1 (Early Action IEP)	➤ This form will be shared with parents and other professionals. ➤ Collect key information on the form and make the form an actual teaching tool, for example, ask for 'three areas of strengths' or 'three areas of concern'. Invite staff to consider their concerns within the context of developmental milestones. ➤ Include information about what you have done to help and other sources of support. ➤ Make sure that parents' views are also collected and, if appropriate, those of the child, too.
Form 2 (review of IEP)	Make the IEP and review of IEP forms lead easily from one to the other and state how staff will learn to use them.

Change action plan

Action needed	Who will do this?	What resources will be needed? (training/finance/time)	Communication methods (as many ways as possible and as often as possible)	Possible problem	Possible solution

Manager's change check-list

Questions	Yes	No	How do I know?
Have I checked that everyone knows why we are making the change?			
Does everyone know the benefits of the change?			
Does everyone know how it will affect them?			
Can everyone answer the question 'What is in it for me?'?			
Is the action plan working?			
Is there enough communication? Have I missed anyone?			
Am I coping with the change myself? Do I need help?			
Am I checking progress weekly? Am I asking the right questions and getting useful feedback?			
What else do I need to consider?			

Self-assessment of performance at meetings

➤ How many meetings did you attend this week?

➤ Did you know exactly why you were attending them?

➤ Did you prepare by reading around the subject and the last minutes?

➤ Did you receive an agenda in advance?

➤ Do you feel that the meeting served the intended purpose?

➤ Was it valuable or a waste of time?

➤ Did you know what was expected of you in the meeting?

➤ Did you make a contribution?

➤ Was it informed and clear?

➤ Did the meeting start on time?

➤ Did it finish on time?

➤ Was the meeting too long or too short?

➤ Do you feel that everyone participated fairly?

➤ Did everyone sum up, so that you had a clear understanding of the action points?

➤ Have you received the minutes yet?

➤ Are they clear and easy to read?

➤ Do you know what action you need to take?

➤ Could you identify two things that you learned from the meeting?

➤ Have you considered how you will share the information and with whom?

Use your answers to identify what you do well at meetings and what worries you about meetings, so that you can identify what skills you need to develop to improve your ability to participate, lead and manage meetings.

OFSTED inspection preparation plan

This is a summary of the key evidence that will need to be demonstrated during an OFSTED inspection of a daycare setting. This will be in addition to the OFSTED inspector's report who will observe practice, check the environment and look at staff records of training. Use this form to help you collect relevant evidence to demonstrate to the inspector.

Standard 1 – Suitable person	
Evidence required	Example of evidence
Staff vetting procedure, to check suitability and that manager is fit for the job. Staff's experience and qualification.	Equal opportunities in recruitment and selection processes, police checks, health checks, reference take-up policy. All staff members' job descriptions, roles and responsibilities. Staff training programme and appraisals.

Standard 2 – Organisation	
Evidence required	Example of evidence
Deployment of staff.	Shift rota, outings policy, indoor and outdoor arrangements. Non-contact time.
Size of group of children (not to exceed 26).	Key-worker system.
Staff training.	As above, plus induction programmes.
Registration.	Register and systems for checking the children's attendance.
Staff ratios.	How you meet the ratio requirements. Arrangements for cover.
Operational plan.	Planning system, rota, routine.

Standard 3 – Care, learning and play	
Evidence required	Example of evidence
The individual needs of the children are met, to promote confidence, independence and self-esteem.	Personal, social and emotional policy. Activity plans. Rules of the setting. Routine. Circle time. Individual educational plans. Last OFSTED inspection report.

Standard 4 – Physical environment	
Evidence required	Example of evidence
Premises are safe, secure and suitable.	Health and safety policy. Health and safety officer. Environmental health reports. Record of cleaning contract. Available telephones. Premises management systems, including record of repairs and maintenance. Staff's paediatric first-aid certificates. Staff's food-handling certificates. Fire-safety report. Fire-drill records.
Indoor and outdoor play areas.	Toilets (one toilet and hot-and-cold-water hand basin per ten children); separate toilet for adults. Staff room.

PHOTOCOPIABLE

Standard 5 – Equipment	
Evidence required	**Example of evidence**
Suitable use of furniture, equipment and toys for appropriate play. Safety standards are met.	Policy for purchasing equipment. Safety equipment. Portable-appliance test reports. Inspector's observation of equipment. If minibus used, policy regarding safety harnesses, insurance and staff as drivers.

Standard 6 – Safety	
Evidence required	**Example of evidence**
Promotion of safety in the setting and on outings.	Health and safety policy, officer, meetings and training. Risk assessments. Contingency plans for evacuation. Fire-drill books. Accident monitoring. Fire certificates. Outings policy.

Standard 7 – Health	
Evidence required	**Example of evidence**
Promotion of good health and prevention of the spread of infection.	Cleaning contract. Health and safety policy. Food-handling certificates. Administration of medicine procedure. Policy regarding sick children. First-aid box. Paediatric first-aid certificates. Consent forms. No-smoking policy. How you teach the children about health and hygiene.

Standard 8 – Food and drink	
Evidence required	**Example of evidence**
Provision of regular drinks and food for children, which are nutritious and well prepared and which comply with dietary and religious requirements.	Staff's food-handling certificates. Snack time. Water fountain or easy access to water. Menu. List, in kitchen, of the children's food allergies. Information on packed lunch. Training for cooks where appropriate.

Standard 9 – Equal opportunities	
Evidence required	**Example of evidence**
Promotion of equality of opportunity and anti-discriminatory practice.	Equal opportunities in recruitment and selection process for all staff. Equal opportunities policy. Managing diversity statement. Parents' handbook. Admission procedure.

Manager's handbook *early years* **training & management**

Standard 10 – Special needs (including SEN and disabilities)	
Evidence required	Example of evidence
Awareness of special needs and compliance with the special needs policy.	Special needs policy. Proof of qualified SENCO. SENCO support group. Individual education plans.
Standard 11 – Behaviour	
Evidence required	Example of evidence
Management of a wide range of children's behaviour in a way that promotes their welfare and development.	Personal, social and emotional policy. Special needs policy. Child protection policy. Allegations of abuse against staff policy. Incident records. Rules of the setting.
Standard 12 – Working in partnership with parents and carers	
Evidence required	Example of evidence
Partnership of parents and carers.	Parents' handbook and information pack. Complaints procedure. Parents' board. Newsletters. Parents' evenings and meetings. Parents' representative and associated information. Confidentiality policy.
Standard 13 – Child protection	
Evidence required	Example of evidence
Child protection.	Child protection policy. Record of relevant training. Statement in parents' handbook. Statement on admissions form.
Standard 14 – Documentation	
Evidence required	Example of evidence
Records, policies and procedures.	Operational handbook. Children's records and archiving procedures (documents held for two years).
Annex A – Babies and children under two	
Evidence required	Example of evidence
Care of babies.	Baby policy. Baby procedures. Baby planning. Relevant records of staff training.

Evaluation of teaching and learning

This form is designed to support your staff when considering the effectiveness of teaching methods and learning strategies with regards to helping each child reach their potential.

Area of Learning to be evaluated and relevant Early Learning Goals (topic, scheme of work, period of time and so on)
What were the planned learning outcomes?
What teaching strategies were used and why?
What were the strengths of the teaching approaches? (give examples)
What were the weaknesses of the approaches? (give examples)
How did the teaching strategies affect the children's attitudes to learning?

PHOTOCOPIABLE

Manager's handbook early years *training & management*

Evaluation of the service

This form is designed to help your staff complete a short evaluation of the overall service. The information could be analysed and used at the staff meeting to identify the staff members' perceptions of the service, the areas that need improvement, and training and resource gaps.

Consider the quality of the following. Is it good and are there areas for improvement?	Yes	No	Comments
Adult–children relationships			
Children's involvement in the activities			
Children's behaviour			
Quality of engagement between staff and children			
Sense of achievement and pleasure from staff, children and parents			
Quality and balance of activities across the range of curriculum areas			
Way that we build and extend children's curiosity			
Differentiation, including appropriate challenges			
Inclusion strategies as part of a topic and routine planning			
Any other area?			

PHOTOCOPIABLE

Bibliography

- Adair, John. *Effective Leadership Masterclass*. Pan, 1997.
- Camacho, L, and P Paulus, 'The Role of Anxiousness in Group Brainstorming'. *Journal of Personality and Social Psychology* 68 (1995).
- Drucker, Peter. *Management Challenges for the 21st Century*. Butterworth Heinemann, 1999.
- Eyre, E C. *Mastering Basic Management*. Palgrave Macmillan Publishers, 1982.
- Fearns, Peter. *Business Studies, Teach Yourself* series, 6th ed. Hodder and Stoughton Educational, 2001.
- Handy, Charles. *Understanding Organisations*. 4th ed. Penguin, 1992.
- Heller, Robert. *Managing Change*. Dorling Kindersley, 1998.
- Honey, Peter, and Alan Mumford. *The Manual of Learning Styles*. Peter Honey Publications, 1982.
- Honey, Peter, and Alan Mumford. *Using Your Learning Styles*. Peter Honey Publications, 1986.
- Howells, Richard, and Brenda Barrett. The Health and Safety at Work Act: A Manager's Guide. Institute of Personnel Management, 1982.
- Huczynski, Andrzej, and David Buchanan. *Organizational Behaviour: An Introductory Text*, 4th ed. Financial Times Prentice Hall, 2000.
- Kermally, Sultan. *Management Tool Kit*. Thorogood, 1999.
- Maslow, Abraham. 'A theory of Human Motivation'. *Psychological Review* 50 (1943): 370-396.
- McCalman, James, and Robert A Paton. *Change Management: A Guide to Effective Implementation*. Paul Chapman Publishing, 1992.
- Peters, Tom. *Thriving on Chaos: Handbook for a Management Revolution*. Pan, 1989.
- Pettinger, R. *Introduction to Management*, 3rd ed. Palgrave Macmillan, 2002.
- Price, A St John, *Understand Your Accounts*. Kogan Page, 1999.
- Randell, Gerry, P Packard and J Slater. *Staff Appraisal: A First Step to Effective Leadership*. Institute of Personnel Management, 1984.
- Rodd, Jillian. *Leadership in Early Childhood*, 2nd ed. Open University Press, 1998.
- Rumbold, Angela. *Starting with Quality: Report of the Committee of Inquiry into the Quality of the Educational Experience Offered to Three- and Four-year-olds*. Her Majesty's Stationery Order for the Department of Education and Science, 1990.
- Stanton, Nicky. *Mastering Communication*, 3rd ed. Palgrave Macmillan Publishers, 1996.
- Stranks, Jeremy. *A Manager's Guide to Health and Safety at Work*, 6th ed. Kogan Page, 2001.
- Torrington, Derek, and Laura Hall. *Human Resource Management*, 4th ed. Financial Times Prentice Hall, 1998.
- Tuckman, Bruce. 'Development Sequence in Small Groups'. Psychological Bulletin (63b) (1965): 384-399.